POWER MOVES

MAKE YOUR MOVE

THE POWER MOVES TOUR

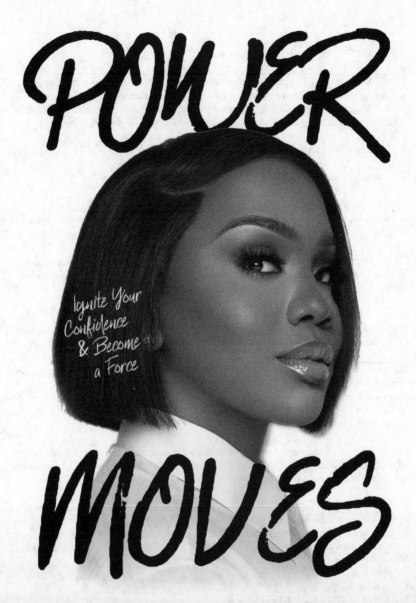

POWER MOVES

Ignite Your Confidence & Become a Force

SARAH JAKES ROBERTS

W PUBLISHING GROUP

An Imprint of Thomas Nelson

Published in Nashville, Tennessee, by W Publishing, an imprint of Thomas Nelson.

The author is represented by the Dupree Miller Agency.

Thomas Nelson titles may be purchased in bulk for educational, business, fundraising, or sales promotional use. For information, please email SpecialMarkets@ ThomasNelson.com.

Unless otherwise noted, Scripture quotations are taken from the New King James Version®. Copyright © 1982 by Thomas Nelson. Used by permission. All rights reserved.

Scripture quotations marked ESV are taken from the ESV® Bible (The Holy Bible, English Standard Version®). Copyright © 2001 by Crossway, a publishing ministry of Good News Publishers. Used by permission. All rights reserved.

Scripture quotations marked NIV are taken from The Holy Bible, New International Version®, NIV®. Copyright © 1973, 1978, 1984, 2011 by Biblica, Inc.® Used by permission of Zondervan. All rights reserved worldwide. www.Zondervan.com. The "NIV" and "New International Version" are trademarks registered in the United States Patent and Trademark Office by Biblica, Inc.®

Grateful acknowledgment is made for permission to reproduce from the following: Marianne Williamson, *A Return to Love: Reflections on the Principles of "A Course in Miracles"* (San Francisco: HarperOne, 2009).

Any internet addresses, phone numbers, or company or product information printed in this book are offered as a resource and are not intended in any way to be or to imply an endorsement by Thomas Nelson, nor does Thomas Nelson vouch for the existence, content, or services of these sites, phone numbers, companies, or products beyond the life of this book.

ISBN 978-0-7852-9190-9 (HC)
ISBN 978-0-7852-9193-0 (audiobook)
ISBN 978-0-7852-9192-3 (ePub)
ISBN 978-0-7852-9190-9 (ITPE)

Library of Congress Control Number: 2023945443

Printed in the United States of America

24 25 26 27 28 LBC 5 4 3 2 1

This book is dedicated to any person who wonders if they are enough. May you discover the power in being yourself and release the gift of you every place you go.

CONTENTS

CONTENTS

Our deepest fear is not that we are inadequate.
Our deepest fear is that we are powerful beyond measure.
It is our light, not our darkness, that most frightens us.
We ask ourselves,
Who am I to be brilliant, gorgeous, talented, fabulous?
Actually, who are you *not* to be?
You are a child of God.
Your playing small doesn't serve the world.
There's nothing enlightened about shrinking
so that other people won't feel insecure around you.
We are all meant to shine, as children do.
We were born to make manifest the
glory of God that is within us.
It's not just in some of us;
it's in everyone.
And as we let our own light shine,
we unconsciously give other people
permission to do the same.
As we're liberated from our own fear,
our presence automatically liberates others.

MARIANNE WILLIAMSON

INTRODUCTION

I'M NOT SURE WE SPEND ENOUGH TIME TALKING ABOUT HOW QUICKLY our power can be stripped away. Often, we don't even feel it when it happens. Like a pickpocket on a bustling street, one encounter with rejection, betrayal, systemic oppression, pain, or fear can leave our souls with a vacancy that power was meant to fill. Out of desperation we cling to external markers of power. Status—whether it be relational, financial, professional—or notoriety masquerade as fillers for the place where our soul is now empty.

The only thing worse than being powerless is falling for the illusion that power can be amassed by what you have instead of who you are willing to become. One of the earliest definitions of power dates to the thirteenth century. It is defined as the "ability to act or affect something strongly."[1] The circumstances that have affected your ability are not puny opponents. They have real power.

If you have ever found yourself withdrawing and isolating because you're confused, doubtful, or nervous, it's not because you are weak. It's evidence that your power is under attack. For most of us it was taken before we even realized how precious it was. When we experience distress, it doesn't just wound us; it robs us. It drains us of power before we can even patch the hole.

You might be able to acknowledge that you have been changed by that theft. You may agree that you have been drained. But did you know that you don't have to accept this inwardly frustrated state you're in? The reclamation of your power is an act of defiance. Your days of faking it until you make it are over.

You're finally ready to acknowledge that you have been grasping for confidence, strength, and joy to no avail. No, I'm going to serve you into facing off with the ideologies, memories, oppression, and fears that have turned you into a shell of who you know you can be and declare to them and for yourself that power moves.

That trauma does not get to keep your power hostage. Shame does not get to hold your tongue. Rejection cannot stifle your creativity. Fear cannot dictate your destiny. People-pleasing cannot hijack your authenticity. It may have had the power to rob you of your yesterday, but it doesn't get to have another second of your destiny.

There is not a message I am more passionate about right now than the fluidity of power. I want us to do more than acknowledge the power of what has limited us. I want us to recognize that power can be restored. My life has been marked by the evidence of this truth. My relationship with God has awakened me to more than just a life of penance and remorse. I have discovered that dry bones can live again, joy does come in the morning, and abundant life exists after heartbreak.

I am going to share with you what I've learned about reclaiming and redefining power. It is going to be liberating in ways you didn't even realize you needed, and the best part of it all is that it won't require you to pretend. A truly powerful existence cannot be built on a lie. So the only request I have is honesty. There will be moments when these words require reflection.

The truth that surfaces may not be something you're ready for anyone else to hear. That's okay. Where you start may not be where you land, but until you learn to make space for your truth, you cannot tap into the fullness of God's goodness concerning your life, nor can you reasonably expect anyone else to do the same. I'm honored to be your guide on this journey of reclamation. I've already prayed that God would grant me wisdom, insight, and clarity to lead you back to power. You won't believe how much more there is to you than this.

CHAPTER 1

CLAMPED DOWN

I WANT TO START BY SAYING, IF YOU'RE ONE OF THOSE PEOPLE WHO know better and *instantly* do better, I'm probably going to be that person in your friend circle whom you roll your eyes at constantly. It's okay. Everyone has one, two, or maybe three of those types of friends. You need us in your life. We keep you humble. If you're not one of those people and you have the ability to know something but need to let it marinate before you activate it in your life, then welcome home! I am your people.

Over time many things in my life have moved from the marination stage into the activation stage. For example, I didn't just become someone who enjoyed working out four to five times a week. I got to a stage in my life where the articles I read about health and fitness made it clear that the key to overall wellness would require that cardio and strength training become a part of my lifestyle. Did I close the article, grab running shoes, and never look back? I did no such thing. I had to let it marinate for a little while before activating it into my habits.

Sometimes, when I shop online, I load up my cart with things I like but not necessarily things I will buy. After I'm finished perusing the site, I go look at the cart, my total, and bank account and then determine what, if anything, will actually be coming to my doorstep. Do you think that those items are just sitting in my cart doing nothing? Of course not—they're marinating.

My "marinating before activating" theory is how I sized up therapy before actually reaching out to a professional. It's the same way I ruminate on tough conversations before actually bringing them up. I don't even make a hair decision before letting it marinate first. There are many things that have been activated in my life as a result of marination before activation.

Anyone who knows their way around the kitchen knows that marinating is not required, but for the right recipes it can make a huge difference. When meat or veggies are marinating, they are placed in a combination of oil, seasoning, spices, and sauces to add flavor or to tenderize the meat. When time is short and preparation is a luxury, I don't have the time to play *Top Chef* in the kitchen. But when I do have the bandwidth and I want the results of my time in the kitchen to be memorable, I take the time to create a marinade.

When it comes to life decisions, I need time to sit with ideas before allowing them to transform my identity. I take the time to ponder them in my heart and to examine what ways I will have to grow in order for the idea to become a tangible truth that can activate a healthier version of myself. There have been many instances in the past when I have set out to cook a new dish that required marination and overestimated my availability and energy. Sometimes the meat stayed sealed in a bag for longer than I anticipated, but the extra time worked in my favor and the meat was infused with even richer flavor.

Then there are occasions when ordering in or cooking something fast and easy makes more sense than the culinary experience I have in mind. I leave the meat to marinate but it inevitably goes bad, and I choose comfort and ease over what could have been an adventure for my taste buds. The same thing happens when concepts that can transform my identity, expression, and relationships are marinating. The results are either an adventure that yields beautiful change or a commitment to choosing ease over braving the unknown. I have a few things that are stuck in the marination phase for me right now, and only time will tell if I'll find the courage and energy to move them into activation.

One of the things marinating right now has to do with a décor decision for our bedroom. I've read a few different blogs that all say we should be utilizing our bedroom exclusively as a place for rest or adult time. Have you heard that? Essentially, you should avoid using your bedroom for taking meetings, responding to emails, watching television, or, umm . . . writing books.

Evidently when your bedroom is reserved for sleeping or sexy time, it trains your mind and body to disassociate from the stresses of life and work. The concept makes perfect sense in theory. As long as my children live in the house with me, however, my chances for privacy outside my bedroom are slimmer than I was in 2013. Therefore, that novel idea will stay in the marination stage for the foreseeable future. I can tell you right now there's no way I'd be able to finish this book or an episode of *Bridgerton* if I adhered to that rule.

My commitment to having a television in my husband, Touré's, and my bedroom taught me a valuable lesson about how so many lose touch with power without even realizing it. A couple of years ago we moved into a rental home. My priority is usually getting it set up in the first day or so so that we're settled enough to rest and shower with minimal stress. Still, it doesn't quite feel like home until the television is set up. Fortunately, at the new house the owners said it was easier for them to leave the television in our bedroom than dismount it and patch the wall where it was hanging.

A few months into living in the home, we hopped in bed after a long day. We were ready to unwind with an episode of our favorite show. I grabbed the remote and pointed it to the television. Nothing happened. I exchanged the batteries in the remote with fresh batteries from a different controller. I extended my arm and pressed Power again. The black screen didn't budge.

My husband took it as a sign that we should rest and started snoozing. I was not so easily converted. I waved my arms around like a conductor at the philharmonic while I attempted to find the right angle to bring the television to life.

Eventually I got out of the bed and unplugged the TV, and then plugged it back in. Pressed the button on the actual device. Nothing. As a last resort I grabbed my husband's clippers out of his suitcase and tested the outlet. Maybe the breaker needed to be switched or a circuit was blown. The clippers began to hum as soon as I clicked them on. Since I didn't buy the TV I had no idea whether it was still under warranty or had a history of malfunctioning.

Through a process of elimination, I could confidently say that the problem wasn't the remote and it wasn't the outlet. The problem was happening inside the television. We travel and work so much that our TV time had become more of a treat than a routine, and it was impossible to gauge when it had stopped working. All I know is that somewhere along the way the TV went from being the main attraction in the room to nothing more than a dark screen taking up space on the wall.

A FORCE IN THE MAKING

What was so interesting about the TV no longer working was that it's not that it lacked power. The power was flowing, but there was something internally keeping the TV from converting the power into function.

If you've ever been in a room or environment and felt incapable of demonstrating confidence, then you may be more like the busted TV than you realize. If we could peek inside your thoughts in those moments, we'd see that you're not without ideas to contribute or a perspective to share, but you can't figure out how to get what's in you out of you.

This could happen when being introduced to a new social circle, contributing in a work environment, or even engaging in intimate relationships. When you are unable to connect the dots between who you sense you could become and who you presently are, it doesn't just cause internal frustration—it renders you powerless.

You don't defend yourself when misunderstood. You don't trust that your perspective can add value. You downplay your ideas and convince yourself that maintaining the status quo is better than introducing something new. You allow the things you believe you can make better to stay the same, and as a result you're not the only one rendered powerless, and your environment is less potent too.

Fortunately there's a secret advantage to being like that television that should give you a sense of relief. It would have been a major headache if there were faulty wires in the wall of the home that needed to be replaced or some other electrical issue hindering the flow of power. But the television had access to power. The issue was with the device, which meant our focus could be directed to converting the power it had access to, to power it to come back to life.

You're probably thinking, *That's great for the TV, but what does that have to do with me?* You either have access to power but not conversion or no access at all. Here's a spoiler alert you won't mind knowing: there's no such thing as no access to power. Your breath is evidence that power is still accessible to you.

> " Your breath is evidence that power is still accessible to you. If you have breath, you have access.

If you have breath, you have access. But until we go within and figure out what's not functioning properly, we can't take advantage of the access to power that we possess.

Did you play with a water hose on a hot day as a kid? It's a fun way to stay cool and keep kids busy that my parents turned to quite frequently. I'm not sure if your water hose was as fancy as ours, but when we were outside playing, we had two ways to turn the hose on and off. One was by turning the knob on the base of the hose where it connected to the house. Immediately the water would begin to flow. The other way was much more sophisticated and involved grabbing the water hose, folding it together, and stopping the flow. Unsurprisingly, the latter method doesn't work without initiating the first one.

This is a perfect example of what happens to us when the power we have access to ceases to flow into our life. When the power is flowing, it's not much different from water gushing through a water hose at full speed. It moves without restriction. It takes on many different forms without being committed to any particular way of being. When your power is flowing, you have the ability to act or affect something strongly.

In this flow our capacity for what's possible increases and transforms our perspective about ourselves and the lives we've been chosen to live. No wonder we feel blocked when we can't convert that kind of power. Can I offer you a gift that can help to unblock some of what you're experiencing? Right now, in this very moment, power is on and flowing in your direction.

Can you let that sink in? Say this aloud: "Power is flowing in my direction." No matter how much disarray you're experiencing or how dull the routine is that you're trapped in, power is still flowing in your direction. Undoubtedly, there may be something clamping down on the flow, but doesn't it feel good to know that power is closer than it appears? If you're struggling to accept that as truth, it's okay. Just let it marinate for now.

There is something about the way you are presently wired that is keeping the power you have access to from converting into the confident, resilient, and bold person you desire to become. I'm going to help you untangle the wires that make you feel like you're short-circuiting when you should be moving with intentionality, authority, and confidence.

I know you're probably ready to roll up your sleeves and dismantle the obstacle standing in the way of you being powerful. What if it's not *something* that is in the way, but *someone*? Until we discover what beliefs, or lack thereof, are clamping your flow, you will have temporary bursts of power but nothing sustainable. The vicious cycle of feeling like you're moving in the right direction and then suddenly slung a thousand feet back will continue until you stop trying altogether or do the work of this book.

I know we're just warming up here, but I want to drop a truth bomb that will open you up to fully receive all that this message offers. Your power is not going to come from an opportunity, position, or person.

Power is an inside job, and you can waste time trying to pursue power from people and things, or you can allow it to accumulate and then erupt from the inside.

Your situation may seem dire and a shift in your environment may absolutely be necessary, but nothing changes until you change. You are in your way. That may seem like a strong statement, but I will unpack it with you. Your loyalty to the way you assume things should be is keeping you from showing up powerfully in the way things are. This in no way absolves the outside forces or systems that may be contributing to your clamped flow, but it should empower you to identify the way you may be giving them a license to stunt your determination and desire.

You are not irreparably broken, incapable, or inadequate. It's not even necessarily the lack of examples in your world. The ultimate limitation you're experiencing is the result of constant internal and external pressure to conform, stay silent, perform, or achieve. If that pressure is not released, it eventually ends up having more power to stop you than you have to break free from it. If you're like me the application of that pressure did not happen overnight or as a result of one particular thing, but it was a slow tightening over time.

By the way, I want to take a moment and simply say, I'm sorry. I know that I may not have applied the pressure you're experiencing. I know I likely didn't play a role in your silent suffering, but still, I'm sorry that you've lost your way. I know what it's like to feel powerless in a world that seems like it's outpacing you. A world where it feels like your truth is better left unspoken. It's scary. It's lonely. The only thing more frightening than being powerless is the fear of how being powerful may disrupt your environment.

> " The only thing more frightening than being powerless is the fear of how being powerful may disrupt your environment.

Don't worry. I'm not going to take you from zero to one hundred. I think you'll find that this approach to reclaiming your power is considerate and not adversarial to the variables you have to navigate. Being powerful does not have to come at the expense of trampling on opportunities and connections that you value. I wholeheartedly believe that you can walk in power, love, humility, and kindness all at the same time. Jesus is a beautiful example of this truth. It's essential that you become discontent with the way things are and hungry for what could be so that we can work together to get you to the most powerful you.

With each turn of a page, you will feel yourself reclaiming strength, confidence, creativity, and vision. You're going to break through what has limited you—armed with the power to never be limited again. You are not meant to be a broken fixture in your world that resembles something familiar and useful but is just taking up space. You're a force in the making.

COURAGEOUSLY AUTHENTIC

Let's lay some groundwork first, shall we? There is no breakthrough without breakdown. This moment carries breakthrough for you. I've prayed that God would give me divine wisdom and insight on how to awaken you to what disrupted your ability to be a channel for power. That's where the breakdown comes into play. It's time for you to fully step into the powerful being He had in mind when He decided the world needed your imprint.

In laying out the road map to lead you to the powerful version of yourself, I realize that it could feel overwhelming to do an overhaul of your life. We're going to take this step-by-step. We'll analyze where you experienced a breakdown between your most powerful self and the fixture on the wall of your life that you have become.

It would have been nice for me to receive a warning from the television before it died. I would have even taken a flickering picture to let me know that trouble was on the way. At least the electric company sends a notice before it shuts off your power. But there is no notice when you are existing in a situation that will ultimately disconnect you from the power you're supposed to convert into abundant life. It happens so subtly that most of us don't even realize it's happened at all.

There is a wide range of culprits that zap our power. They can be overtly flagrant like heartbreak, abuse, betrayal, and abandonment or inconspicuously draining like the demands of success, productivity, or support for your community. It's much easier to attribute the loss of our power to the big moments that have left us wounded, but the subtle paper cuts that rob us along the way can be just as damaging.

The loss of power shows up in different ways for everyone. Here are a few signs that can indicate you're experiencing a loss of power:

- You find yourself habitually conforming to ideas that contrast sharply with what you really want or believe.
- You feel enraged when asked to fulfill obligations that you set the precedent to complete.
- You feel resentful at other people's ability to freely express themselves.
- You find yourself overreacting to trivial issues.
- You feel a constant longing and discontentment.
- You choose appeasing others over advocating for yourself.
- You feel trapped inside your life, regardless of how many things should be a source of joy.
- You feel annoyed when people speak, especially incorrectly, on your behalf or about you in your presence.

For many of us feeling powerless is something that happens over time. No one is born powerless. As a matter of fact, the opposite is true. From the moment you were an embryo in your mother's womb, you began disrupting things. Smells began to make her ill. Her clothing had to give way to make room for your growth. She tossed and turned for comfort because you unapologetically took up space.

I firmly believe that we all enter the world with that innate power to be a force. If you don't believe me, go visit the home of a new parent.

There's no power struggle going on in that household. The newborn is running the show. She is determining when the adult sleeps, showers, eats, sits, stands, talks on the phone, and so on.

It has been said in my community that part of what makes babies so precious is that in the early stages of their lives they are more divine than they are human. Their innocence, power, and confidence have not yet been diluted by the realities of life. It's not until the parent hits rock bottom and revolts against the shock of newborn life that the baby begins to realize that her power is in competition with other factors.

The newborn stage is the beginning of a lifelong power struggle that ensues for us all, but there's a steady stream of different opponents. Family members, classmates, friends, societal norms, lovers, traditions, coworkers, systems, and bosses all tag team along with their expectations and divide your confidence, focus, and vision. Eventually you feel like that newborn who is no longer running the show. Only this time you're an adult on the stage of life trying to make it to the next scene.

Now is not the time to lament over the power you've lost. This is an opportunity to acknowledge and accept that the loss of power can be a gift. It makes space for you to reconnect to our all-powerful God who refills, restores, and refuels you in the place where you experienced loss. The dilemma, then, is not how we take up space and make demands on ourselves and others so that our authentic self can come back to life. Our journey is about returning to an uninhibited version of ourselves who are not in a struggle *for* power, because we know that the ability to be authentic in a world that thrives off conformity is power. I'm going to help you tap into the courage to live authentically.

BACKED BY POWER

The creation story in Genesis 1 tells us that when God created man and woman, He made them in His own image. Given that God does not have physical form, the only image that we could possibly bear that resembles our Creator must be an inner image—our spirit. I'll be the first to say that my insides don't look nothing like God's. Instead, my insides are like a melting pot bearing the image of all the prayers, fears, hopes, painful memories, dreams, and nagging insecurities that I have.

I know not many people are comfortable admitting this truth, but I've met enough people to know that my insides are not the only messy interiors on this planet. Yours are too. All of us are messy in some way, but not all of us embark on the journey of trusting that there is power in our mess. Genesis 3 chronicles the gateway responsible for our messy insides in great detail. It depicts the story of confusion that clamped the flow of power that God desired His creation to freely receive from Him. In exchange, a counterfeit version of power was introduced.

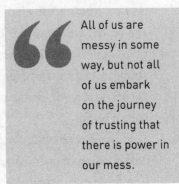

All of us are messy in some way, but not all of us embark on the journey of trusting that there is power in our mess.

You've probably heard it before. A serpent deceived the woman into believing that God would be jealous of her if she possessed as much knowledge as God. This convinced her to eat from a forbidden tree. The woman enticed the man to do the same. As a result of eating from the tree, their power moved from accomplishing what God set out for them to hiding behind their fears. They became more focused on themselves than on God. Whenever we become more self-conscious than God-conscious, pressure is applied to our flow of power.

Every generation born after the man and woman would be tasked with cleaning up that mess, while making new messes along the way. Making a commitment to declutter generational messiness is a daunting task, but it's also the beginning of power flowing again. You do not have to be a victim of the same circumstances that thwarted someone in your family from being powerful.

Just because someone chose to stay silent, pretend, conform, or hide doesn't mean that their life is the template. You do not have to campaign for your autonomy. Being courageous is not a team sport. When life affords us the opportunity to embark on a journey of change as a collective, it is beautiful. There are few things more tragic, however, than staying the same because you are afraid to change alone.

When one person cleans up even one corner of their messy lives, they break a link on the chain that has prohibited generations from experiencing the freedom that comes with growing in power. What occurred in Genesis 3 was a departure from God's intention for us to reflect the strength of His Spirit on the earth. Before that fateful moment in the garden occurred, Genesis 1 lets us know messy insides are not what God had in mind.

God envisioned a human experience that didn't require inner work before outer impact. When He created humanity, we were released to be a force instantaneously. He used big words like *subdue* and *dominion*.

"And God blessed them. And God said to them, 'Be fruitful and multiply and fill the earth and subdue it, and have dominion over the fish of the sea and over the birds of the heavens and over every living thing that moves on the earth'" (Genesis 1:28 ESV).

Why would God use such powerful words unless He knew in His plan that they could access the power necessary to fulfill that charge? When God gave them the command, it didn't require them to work through their nerves, doubts, abandonment issues, or perfectionism. Those are all things we confront now before we can even consider God's perfect plan for our imperfect lives. You know why He did not need to untangle their thoughts from His thoughts? Because they were meant to be so perfectly made in God's image that their thoughts were His thoughts. Their ways were His way. The DNA of their insides bore the fingerprints of God's power.

I won't lie, if we're self-aware, when we embrace the notion that our insides were meant to bear the image of God's character, it can be discouraging. Because we know how far off we are from being anything like God. The distance, though expansive, is not insurmountable. There have been moments in my life when I know for sure that my heart was perfectly aligned with God's and change happened in me and through me. In those moments I knew that the Holy Spirit made up the difference between my doubt and God's abundance.

Each day grants us another opportunity to get closer to reflecting God's image. It doesn't matter what decisions you made yesterday. If you stay alive for one minute past this moment, that's one minute that can be used to bear God's image and reflect His heart to every person you encounter.

Maybe you're tired right now. You believe that the only way you can truly show up for others in a way that represents God is by saying yes to everything even when you don't have what it takes. Let me just remind you of the few times when you prayed that God would do something but He didn't do it. Telling someone no doesn't mean that you don't love them. It simply means that your no has taken into consideration things that they can't even see or perhaps understand.

We can't rightfully determine the external variables that have clamped you down until you're willing to acknowledge the fears that you think change will bring. Your fears have the power to keep you stuck, but the beginning of disarming that fear is when you dare to confront it with intention.

Flip the Switch

Earlier we talked about how I marinate on things before I activate them in my life. Marination is when I begin to consider the pivot I need to make, and the moment of activation is when I flip the switch on.

As much as I'd like you to be able to dive right in to being your most confident, powerful self, I also know that lasting change takes time, and a little marination ain't never hurt nobody. This moment of reflection is how we will lay the foundation for you to become your most powerful self. You can expect to see it at the end of each chapter. Take the time to marinate for as long as you need, but once you sense you're ready, activate and observe how moving in the opposite direction of your fears fills you with power.

When you engage in the work, you will begin the journey of realigning your focus, thoughts, and energy to your authenticity and allowing it to overflow into your purpose, personal community, and ambitions. For now this work is an inside job between you and God.

MARINATE

What are you afraid will happen if the power you long for becomes the power you embody?

ACTIVATE

Reflect on a powerless moment you experienced in your day. What would choosing power have looked like? Do that next time!

PRAY

God, awaken me to the ways Your perfect love can lead me from a place of fear to a place of power.

CHAPTER 2

CAN AGAIN

DISCUSSIONS SURROUNDING WHAT'S AN ADEQUATE AMOUNT OF water for a person to drink vary. Most of my life I heard eight to ten cups a day, then I started hearing half your body weight in ounces. Now the overachievers have me toying with the idea that we must drink a gallon a day. All of us should be drinking our water and, for extra credit, we should be minding our business too. No matter what formula you use for your water consumption, the advantages of hydration are undeniable.

Still, half of you need to pause what you're doing and grab a cup of water. Dehydration wreaks havoc on the body in every way imaginable. If you go without consistent water intake, there comes a point when simply drinking water can't regulate your system.

This is because water alone can't immediately replenish the essential minerals and vitamins that have been depleted. It's ironic because even though the water is getting in your system, it's not enough to actually bring your body to health. Instead, a deeper method of hydration administered through an IV must be utilized to restore the body's optimal functionality.

It's similar to what happens when we discover we are searching for power in the areas where we are deficient. We can become so deeply disconnected from what it means to have true power that the day-to-day moments that should refuel and recharge us slip by unnoticed. Anybody ever woke up tired after sleeping all night? It's because you need more than sleep; your heart, mind, and soul need *rest*. When we enter a state of constant powerlessness, it's not enough to receive a one-off affirmation or validation. We need a deeper infusion that gets to our core and strengthens the *area* where we feel fragility.

Notice how I used the word *area*? It is uncommon that we have power deficiency in every area of our lives, but the areas where we sense underperformance dominates our perception of our overall performance. Let's do a little exercise.

Imagine with me you're standing in an empty parking lot with reserved spaces. You can't tell what each space is labeled, but each time a new expression of your identity is added, a car pulls into a spot. Eventually you see that there are spots labeled child, friend, sibling, partner, leader, student, entrepreneur, or colleague. Each spot with its own car. When you are navigating the responsibilities of your life, you're moving from one vehicle to the next. You leave your leadership car, which is full of gas, and hop into your friendship vehicle, only to see it's out of gas.

You had enough power to galvanize your team towards success, but you don't have the power to admit to your friend that you haven't found a way to introduce who you're becoming into your dynamic. You feel like a bad person because you can't be the kind of friend that you know she needs. In reality, you're neither a bad person nor a bad friend. You've simply run out of the capacity to be the friend she once knew.

Often we chalk our awkward feeling to something we can overpower; eventually it breeds annoyance and resentment in an area where we once had intimacy and joy. When the mere thought of having an encounter with someone deflates you, take the time to work through how your connection with them requires that you disconnect from yourself. Pushing past those moments is how we give license for their expectation of us to be more powerful than our authenticity. Even more problematic than this is how we allow the loss of power in one area of our expression to deduce the ways we're making progress in another.

The need to be refueled in one space does not equate to an overall powerless existence. Additionally, avoiding where we feel powerless doesn't make it go away.

Most of the time we're all navigating the reality that we're strong in one space but weak in another. That's actually why being powerless can be so debilitating. When you have experienced your ability to execute and deliver in one space but have been stagnant in another, it's frustrating. Too often we settle for only functioning in expressions where power comes easily and refueling is not a mystery.

Not this time though. We're going to take the time to celebrate where you experience a steady, affirming flow of power, but also get under the hood to examine the places where you just can't seem to get going. If you can consume affirmations, take a nap, read a scripture, unplug, sign up for adventure, or view a message to get motivated, then you should feel comfort. You have found a formula that fills you again once power is decreasing.

When your power tank has a hole in it, though, those methods don't work as well. They uncover and directly speak to the place where we feel weak, but far too often it's only a temporary power surge that depletes us almost as quickly as it charged us. What do we do when we're so depleted that nothing seems to motivate us any longer?

Some of you can relate. Regardless of how many powerful messages, thoughts, and friends you may be surrounded by, they have been in-efective in sustaining the level of confidence you desire to possess. Have you ever noticed that you legitimately feel determined and focused in the moment, but once you're no longer in the environment, you go back to feeling restricted again?

That's how you know that you need something deeper than just soaking up the power around you. You need to acknowledge where power is leaking from you. I like the parking lot analogy because it speaks to the multidimensional expressions we possess as humans, but it also liberates us from feeling like every area of our life is struggling. If you considered all the reserved spots you occupy as one person with many expressions and checked the power tank on each of them, you may learn that you're not depleted everywhere.

Instead, the areas where you're feeling least fulfilled are affecting you so significantly that they're detracting from courage and confidence in other places. This is an opportunity for you to examine what's happening in those areas that is blocking the power from flowing to the place you need it the most. It's not enough to immerse yourself in power if you can't retain it. You don't just need power to be in you, no more than a car with an empty tank needs a gas canister in the passenger seat. We've got to restore what you need on the inside.

It's important to me that you start with the obligations you deem necessary for yourself: rest, prayer, emotional wellness, physical activity, and all the other things that become "optional" when the demands of life pick up. Have you ever considered why the responsibility we have to our wellness is the first thing we're willing to sacrifice when prioritizing expectation? It's because we've embraced a mentality that makes it more comfortable for us to disappoint ourselves rather than running the risk of disappointing others. You cannot expect others to advocate for the needs that you have made optional.

You need power that emits from your spirit and gives momentum to all that you do. With this analogy in mind, I'm wondering what the gauge on your power tank would read for all of those different ways you show up in your world. To help answer this, I'd like you to take a few minutes to write a list of all the responsibilities you have to yourself and others. Then, beside each item, gauge how empowered you feel to accomplish those obligations. Take note of the areas where you're full. How'd you get there? What is challenging about the places where you feel empty?

The etymology of the word *empower* simply means "in ability."[2] It is when the power you've been exposed to becomes the power that moves you. When God created humankind in His image, their power tank was full. They were loaded with ability. He did not just allow them to live amid the power of the ocean, animals, plants, stars, and sun hoping that the power around them would motivate them.

No, God positioned them not to just see the power around them but to explore the power within. There was no such thing as "I can't," "I shouldn't," or "I don't know how." God charged them in Genesis 1, and that mission, combined with their undiluted sense of being made in His image, was enough for them to turn a charge into an action.

God won't give you an assignment that He will not empower you to accomplish. Who would you be if you leaned into that? What fear would subside and what doubt die if you truly trusted that everything God has assigned for you to accomplish He's also reserved the power for you to get done? God has power on reserve with you in mind. All you have to do is align your heart and mind to receive what's already yours.

Can you just imagine it for a minute? Imagine having a fresh flow of ability. I don't mean fake ability either. You know when you say you are able, but secretly you're resentful because you said yes when you really didn't have it?

No, this is the type of ability that makes completing whatever responsibility is ahead of you effortless. Being powerful doesn't mean that you don't get tired. God introduced the Sabbath for a reason. It does mean you'll no longer feel trapped playing a character that is inauthentic to who you are and what you need. Inauthenticity is the villain of empowerment. God can't empower who you have allowed people to believe you are.

> " Being powerful doesn't mean that you don't get tired.

BREAK UP WITH YOU

When my husband and I first started blending our family, I was nervous to ask my bonus children to do things around the house. I wanted them to think of me as the cool parent who didn't require too much from them. As a result, I would find myself working twice as hard to care for a family of eight as opposed to the work of being a single mom of two.

When my husband charged me with holding them accountable to

the standards I value, even if it was going to be new for them, I resisted. That's actually putting it lightly. I lied and told him, "I actually don't mind. I love serving and taking care of my family." It's true that acts of service are how I show love, but in an effort to build a thick bond with them, I was stretched too thin.

I held on to the narrative for as long as I could until I reached my breaking point. A bond that can thrive only if you're in a perpetual state of overexertion is a hostage situation keeping you from freedom. I dropped the act, found my voice, and I'd like to think added a valuable perspective to their worldview about responsibility and adulthood.

It's difficult to pinpoint the moment you become complicit in denying yourself the ability to be authentic. Just know that whenever you choose to allow someone to settle on a false idea of who you are, then you are embracing an existence that is contingent on inauthenticity. No matter how subtle their misunderstanding may seem, if you allow them to make it truth, then you are accepting a role as an imposter.

It's further complicated when you have been celebrated, esteemed, and acknowledged for who you pretend to be. That's when it becomes even more challenging to figure out who you truly are. You find yourself unable to separate how you truly feel about something from your need to uphold what other people have come to accept and expect from you.

If your opinion is curated with the reaction of other people in mind, then you have been reduced to the equivalent of a ventriloquist's puppet. A false sense of contentment is derived only when you successfully mimic the thoughts and opinions of whoever you desire to please. When this occurs, you unconsciously allow the approval, validation, or acceptance of those you're pleasing to possess more power than you. Your power is not gone; it has simply moved.

It has moved to the people or outcomes you have deemed as more important than showing up as yourself. On the surface it may seem like there is a power struggle taking place, but in reality, a low sense of self-worth is actually the culprit. When you deem yourself as worthy, powerful, intelligent, and valuable, you do not easily cave in to the pressure of who other people believe you should be. I didn't trust that my role as stepmom and my authenticity could live in the same place.

The only reason your power is not present is because you did not believe, or were not aware, that you could possess it in the first place. God told the man and woman that they had dominion, but the serpent convinced them that they could not trust

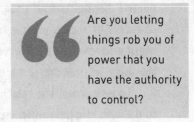

>" Are you letting things rob you of power that you have the authority to control?

what God said. What's crazy about the serpent talking them out of their position of power is that they had power over the very serpent that robbed them. Are you letting things rob you of power that you have the authority to control?

I want you to begin analyzing the ways that you unknowingly relinquish power on small levels. It's easy to think about the big areas that we want to change, but what about the small drains in our lives? The actions and assumptions that poke holes and make way for slow leaks. I have felt powerless before in saving money, losing weight, participating in functions that I did not want to attend, condoning offensive behavior, or allowing someone to blatantly lie in an effort to keep the peace.

I'd told myself that I was incapable of controlling the scenario, but that was never true. I just gave my fear of change more power than my fear of things staying the same. I could have saved the money, but I didn't want my lifestyle to change. I could have lost the weight, but I didn't want my diet to change. I could have said no to the functions, but I didn't want my circle to think differently of me. The fear of change is no longer allowed to hold you hostage.

The more you're willing to open yourself up for change, the more capacity you have for power to flow through you. With God you change your way into power by modeling your life after Jesus. The disciples didn't just drop their fishing nets and receive power. No, they had to walk *with* power before they could walk *in* power. In walking with Jesus they were able to ask questions about what was happening in their spirits and perspectives that was prohibiting them from doing what Jesus did.

A long-lasting love becomes richer and more powerful not because things stayed the same but because two people were able to stay connected throughout all the changes. A friendship that withstands seasons of career changes, relocations, new loves, heartbreaks, and all the other highs and lows of life is a relationship that did not require a person to stay the same in order to remain connected.

To be honest, the relationships that I distance myself from have more to do with the person staying the same than it does with them changing. If you're in my life, I expect for you to change and grow. When I witness my friends taking the awkward, uncomfortable path towards growth, it inspires me. Anyone who needs you to never change is requesting that you never discover who God has destined you to become.

God did not make you in His image for you to limit yourself to one expression of who you are. You are broad, bountiful, nuanced, peculiar, simple, elusive, and blatant just like your Creator. Scripture tells us that God is the same yesterday, today, and forevermore. That means God is consistent, but it doesn't mean God is simple.

You can be consistently authentic and complex at the same time. I have moments when I'm like, "Man, God is so faithful!" and other moments when I'm like, "God, where are you?" It's not because God has changed His character, but rather because God has changed His expression. The most beautiful part of my story has been sitting back to watch and see how God is going to show up next in my life. I just have to remind myself to trust that my search for where or how God is moving will never be in vain.

Throughout the Bible we see how God changed His expression. Sometimes He spoke directly to His creation; other times He used nature to speak to humanity. Then we see Him move through prophet after prophet—still God, new expression. The same all-powerful God made you in His image. A simplified version of you will frustrate your insides because you were empowered for more. I'm not even talking about more material possessions, businesses, or resources. I am not suggesting you're empowered to *get* more. You, my friend, have been empowered to *become* more. You are able to do so much more than you can even comprehend.

NO MORE CAN'T

You know how you see someone doing something totally amazing and think to yourself, *I could never do that.* Speaking in front of a large crowd, embracing their physique, attending an event alone, or acquiring the discipline required to make a change?

We only think we can't do something when we don't have enough personal evidence of a *can't* becoming a *can.* At this point I think my toxic trait is that I think I can do anything—and when I say anything, I mean anything! Build a house? If you give me a book or a YouTube video, I'll figure it out. Disassemble a television and put it back together? Hand me the screwdriver, I got this.

I call it toxic because the house is more than likely going to collapse. But I cannot get out of my head the notion that if someone else has learned to do this, then I can use the same mind God gave me to attempt to get it done myself. I've learned to do too many things that I never thought I'd be able to do, so I am no longer easily convinced that there's something I can't figure out.

Nothing in my life changed until I stopped being *can't* focused and instead became *can* focused. I want you to think about an area in your life where you feel called to something, but you have disqualified yourself with a "can't" for whatever reason. Your can't may be something practical like limited time, finances, or education. It could also be an emotional reason. Write what you want first and then your can't. Here are a few examples:

- I want to write a book, but I can't because I don't know where to start.
- I want to move, but I can't leave everything I've ever known.
- I want to date, but I can't take another heartbreak.

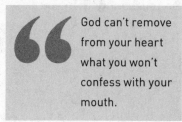

> God can't remove from your heart what you won't confess with your mouth.

Regardless of how you've disguised your want behind a can't, it all has the same sum: your can't has more power than your want. You may be thinking something like, *Yeah, well, not everyone gets what they want.* You're right. But denying what you want means you can't present your truth to yourself, let alone God. If there's something you want that is not aligned with what God has for you, He will teach you how to not want it any longer. God can't remove from your heart what you won't confess with your mouth.

Wanting the same thing as God places you on the same team. Another crazy possibility that you may have never considered is that God wants the same thing for you as you want for yourself. What if the thing you're denying that you want is actually the thing that God has been waiting for you to want? There's a powerful transfer that takes place when we begin to want the same things as God. It is the only way that we are able to truly tap into limitless power or ability for whatever circumstance we're facing.

Have you ever woken up in the morning and realized your phone didn't charge, so you had to accept the low percentage and rely on short windows of charging throughout the day? You can do the same thing in your heart and mind when you're running low on the power you need to face the demands of your day. You're only one prayer away from the recharge you need to feel empowered for the task at hand.

I may not get to have an hour of prayer each morning, but I probably have a collective three hours on the days I wake up drained before I even get out of the bed. That's when I start praying about everything!

Lord, please help me complete the morning school rush with ease.

Lord, give me wisdom on how to navigate my husband's vulnerability.

Lord, help me to navigate this meeting without being frustrated.

By the time my day is over, I know God is probably like, "Here she go again bothering me." It's a funny thought, but I know it's not true because God rejoices in giving us the recharge we need for our day. He delights in His presence being invited into even the smallest detail of our lives.

God has given me wisdom on the spot when having tough conversations with our adult children or even when I'm leading an important meeting with a business partner. Then there are moments when God gives me nothing but peace and patience while He's working out things that I don't yet have an answer for. When you and God are on the same team there will be times when you're on the bench and He's taking the lead.

What a relief it is to know that power is not about feeling strong, intelligent, or full of wisdom, and moving through life with grit. Power is about showing up as your true self even if that version of you is different from who you were yesterday, five years ago, or five minutes ago. Giving yourself permission to stand in your truth doesn't mean that you're right or wrong. It's just truth.

From that place of truth you're able to honor where you are and petition God to reveal where you should be. After spending a lifetime of denying or avoiding my truth in order to pursue acceptance, I've experienced liberation. There is power in being honest with yourself and then sharing that honesty in your relationships with God and others.

You may be wondering, *How do I embark on a journey of identifying what my truth is?* I downloaded a feelings wheel a few years ago because I recognized that my emotional vocabulary was limited. Sometimes it's not that you are actively avoiding how you feel or who you are, but rather that you've never been given the language to accurately identify and express yourself.

My prayer life became much more intimate when I was able to connect the truth of what I was feeling by using specific words like *sorrowful, agitated, insignificant, hopeful, creative, valued*, and so many more. Underneath most of the things we can't do is a feeling we're trying to avoid. Consider our earlier want/can't statements in this light:

- I want to write the book, but I don't think I can survive feeling embarrassed.

- I want to move, but I am nervous about failing or being alone.
- I want to date, but I'm not sure I could survive another disappointment.

You may feel powerless because you have spent more time denying your truth than you have doing the work to understand what you are actively trying to avoid. You probably know a few people who subscribe to the belief system that admitting your truth won't change your reality, so it doesn't matter anyway. You might be one of them. If you've been alive for longer than twelve months, you are well aware that you don't always get what you want. Don't worry, I'm not about to tell you that the moment you identify what you want it will come into your life.

I'm offering you something much more meaningful—the opportunity to not just admit what you want but also to grieve the things you wanted but didn't get to have. Take this opportunity to invite God into a corner of your heart that you rarely visit so that you can release the frustration, anger, tears, and disappointment for not getting what you wanted. Then, because God loves you so much, He'll show you, in that very same space, what He offered you instead. If you can't admit that you wanted it but didn't get it, God can't show you how He made provision for the area where you experienced lack. Power is not just reserved for moving forward. Power is also able to go back and heal what you've tried to leave behind.

Embracing a *can* mentality is not just about giving yourself permission to do something. A can mentality is also giving yourself permission to feel something. I can feel sad. I can feel joy. I can feel ambitious. I can feel tired. I can feel excited. One of the most widely quoted scriptures in the Bible is "I can do all things through Christ who strengthens me" (Philippians 4:13). The apostle who wrote this was not declaring that he could do whatever he wanted but rather acknowledging that with Christ there's no situation that he cannot survive.

Living with the confidence that you can endure hard things makes you resilient. Most of us experience that type of resiliency as children.

Physical pain is easy to overcome, and emotional pain fades almost as quickly as it came—until it doesn't anymore. The loss of the ability to recover is the acceptance of defeat. When we no longer have the power to regenerate resiliency, our decision-making centers around avoiding disappointment or difficult outcomes.

Unknowingly this becomes a part of our core values, and we pursue avoidance over freedom. It's time for you to move your values from what you want to avoid to who you want to become.

Flip the Switch

---- **MARINATE** ----

When do you feel the most powerful? When do you feel the most defeated?

---- **ACTIVATE** ----

Write down the moments when you feel like you can't do something and the reason why you don't think you can.

---- **PRAY** ----

God, help me to dismantle the limits keeping me from being empowered to live out Your vision for my life.

CHAPTER 3

FULLY INTEGRATED

THERE'S A POPULAR FAST-FOOD RESTAURANT KNOWN FOR ITS chicken sandwich, lemonade, and manners. The first time I frequented the restaurant, I paid for my food, then as the team member handed me my order, I offered a casual "Thank you." Before I could fully finish the sentence, they responded, "My pleasure."

This was not an ordinary "my pleasure." No, the way they spoke those two words made me believe for a split second that from the moment they were born and could form words, their lifelong dream was to hand me a spicy chicken sandwich with pepper jack cheese, bacon, and Polynesian sauce on the side.

You would have thought in that moment I was the sole person responsible for their childhood dream becoming a reality. I thought it was a one-off until I went to another location and a different person did the same thing with the same level of sincerity and joy.

As a researcher it became my mission to determine whether every single Chick-fil-A would offer the same response to my gratitude. Twenty-five pounds later and I can report that, for the most part, every time you say "thank you" at the restaurant, you can expect for the team member to respond with "my pleasure."

So accustomed have I become to hearing the two words that when they are not uttered, I feel slightly (okay, deeply) wounded by the lack of pleasure they're taking in handing me my extra sauces. I remember being in a car full of people who kept asking for stuff at the window that they should have requested when I placed the order. (By the way, if you're one of those people, I just want you to know y'all get on the driver's nerves.)

If this were any other establishment, I'd expect some eye-rolling and maybe even some lip-smacking, but not here, because this is the place where it is their pleasure to meet your needs. Well, Chile, listen, on this particular day someone was not in the pleasing mood. By the time we got finished harassing the team member at the window and I'd offered my last apologetic "Thank you," the only thing they could offer back in response was a measly "You're welcome."

That's when I decided to never show my face again at that particular location. We'd blown it! We'd made it so difficult for them that they were in survival mode and abandoned the integrity of the brand. Unlike other restaurants where the integrity of the brand relies on the food having a consistent taste regardless of the location, Chick-fil-A went the extra mile and based their customer experience on the integrity of the overall experience down to what a team member will respond when they hear a customer say the words *thank you*.

I can only imagine what internal structure they have in place to make sure that a consistent customer experience exists at the majority of their restaurants. I'm even more fascinated by the reality that their leadership was intentional about not losing that small, seemingly inconsequential touch even as they experienced growth.

Profitability is a part of the strategy of any business, but you can always tell when it's not the sole driving force behind a business. Chick-fil-A wants to be known for more than food; they also want to be known for faith and kindness. This commitment requires them to consider with intention how faith and kindness show up even when someone is in their drive-through.

Like you're currently doing in your personal life, I'm sure they've undergone evaluating, updating, and deconstructing their internal organization system in the decades they've been in business. Though I'm sure we've frequented Chick-fil-A enough to keep at least one location in business, I am not an insider. I can assume, however, that part of their company evaluations are measured by how well they're maintaining their core values.

Core values are not meant to restrict. Instead, they are the measuring stick that determines whether an idea, opportunity, expansion, or parner ship aligns with the company's founding principles. A fine-dining establishment may change its menu, but I don't think there's ever been one that decided to abandon fine dining in exchange for becoming a fast-food place. That is because one of their core values centers around an elevated culinary experience.

One of the core values of Woman Evolve, an organization that I founded in 2017, is connection. My goal is to create an environment where the women are coming not to be spectators but rather to actively engage in connecting with the women they're having an experience with. Connection robs the Enemy of isolating another person in shame, depression, weariness, or pain. I'm constantly asking myself, How do we make a connection with the women we serve so that they can create meaningful connection with the women in their lives?

When leaders insist that all decisions filter through core values, a company is able to ensure that everything they create reflects what's most important to them as an organization. This commitment is how brand integrity is achieved. I've had to learn a lot about it when creating spaces, products, and services for the women connected with Woman Evolve. There is an expectation of fun, faith, fashion, connection, and undeniable encounters with God that has become synonymous with the experiences we create.

Brand integrity is the foundation that determines how a person or organization will consistently present themselves in the spaces they occupy regardless of how their internal structure may need to be modified.

Four Seasons is a hotel that has built its organization around generous hospitality. They don't always have the most modern hotel concepts, and sometimes they aren't necessarily in the most trendy or convenient parts of a city; however, what you can depend on is that from the moment you're greeted at the door to the moment you check out, their standard of high-level, intentional hospitality has been met.

Now, before you start writing me about that one time you went and you had the worst experience ever, please know that I am speaking in general terms. Their bar for hospitality determines what is acceptable and what is not. It's why when you're sending an email to an organization about a less-than-ideal experience, you are wise to use words like "I know that [insert organization] does not condone this."

Part of the reason this knowing exists is because the company has set a standard of excellence that is the lens through which they're viewed. Of course, there are moments when the company misses the mark, but the mark must be set to begin with so they understand how to recover and regain the trust of their audience.

IT'S PERSONAL

I think one of the challenges we face in igniting our confidence and becoming a force is that we're constantly being told what to value, how to think, what should upset us, how we should feel about our appearance, how we should work, and so much more.

I'm not saying this has happened to me, but I know people who have a collection of supplements that they heard do one thousand different things in the third drawer to the right of their sink all because of scrolling through an app. Also, not saying this is me, but some people are guilty of reading a headline and jumping straight to the comments before they've even formed an informed opinion on a matter. Then, if that's not bad enough, in the moments when they do have an opinion before engaging with the varied perspectives of social media, they find themselves weakening their stances or changing them altogether. Okay, maybe it *is* me, but perhaps it's you too.

I am struck by the reality that a generation is emerging that is wired to consume information but not to marinate in it and determine their own thoughts and opinions about a matter before parroting someone else's perspective. It's not that this didn't exist in previous generations. Our perspectives on politics, ethics, morality, and issues have always been shaped by our social circles.

But it is more pervasive now that our social circle includes the World Wide Web. If you don't know who you are and what you believe, someone else will deposit their views into your experience. I want to help you shape your core values so that you're able to have a lens through which to hold yourself accountable.

This process will aid you in determining what core values should become a staple in your identity—your personal brand. They will serve as the standard for your personal integrity. Core values will determine how you make decisions and who you choose to live life with. I believe that every person should have at least three to five core values that show up in all that they do. A few of my core values, in no particular order, are honor, integrity, accountability, and humility.

The first thing I want you to know is that your specific values may not align with mine. It's likely that we'll have overlap, but our values also differ based on the stages of life we're in. The core values of someone in their twenties versus someone in their sixties may be different. Part of the reason is that there is a cycle of settling and shedding that occurs as we age.

Some principles you settle into so sufficiently that they become a part of your nature. Some convictions you're able to release as you are no longer exposed to the conditions or environments that made them a priority in the first place. I'll give you an example.

At the age of twenty-three, I went through a divorce after four years of marriage. Up until getting divorced I never really thought about my principles. It's difficult to determine what to value when you have been devalued. Once I was divorced, I felt my soul moving into a place of health. The weight of trying was removed and I was left to ask myself the question: Who would you *be* if you weren't being so hard on yourself?

I knew instantly that I wanted to be a good mother and I wanted to be independent.

Intentional motherhood and independence became a part of my core values. Two years after my divorce I met and married my current husband, and one of those values I got to keep, while the other resulted in a wrestling match to pry it out of my hand. Baby, let me tell you something!

There's not a wrestler in a ring that is fiercer than a woman who fought trauma to become independent and now must trust that she's more powerful as a unit than as a lone soldier. Now, let me say this before somebody starts wondering whether the person in their life is worth them laying down their independence.

I became more powerful as a unit with my husband. If the person doesn't make you more powerful, then put your mouthguard in and keep on wrestling, because God does not allow someone to come into your life to make you less. As my husband and I began to build our lives together, I realized that the core value of independence I'd settled into would now have to be shed in order for me to experience how God was showing up for me in a new season of life.

> No weapon formed against you may prosper, but sometimes the values formed in the aftermath of your battle will keep you from prospering.

It was also much easier to give up that principle when I realized that it was a value formed from a place of trauma. No weapon formed against you may prosper, but sometimes the values formed in the aftermath of your battle will keep you from prospering.

Such was the case for me, until I became aware that I was holding on to a value that was keeping me from experiencing the fullness of my husband's and my potential as a unit. The truth is that I'd gotten married and was so focused on the traits I wanted my husband to possess that I never took the time to examine the ones I wanted to hold as a wife.

We are never in a stage of life when we should not be considering what specific values we want to possess in the many roles we may fulfill.

My quest for values begins with my relationship with God. Through prayer, worship, and studying Scripture, I am able to pinpoint what needs to be my priority as I experience the constant transitions of life.

OPEN FOR DEPOSITS

My desire to align my identity with God's intention for my life is a heart posture—that is, a core value that I possess regardless of the environment. When my heart talks to God, it asks, "What do You need me to see and who do You need me to be?" This is how I open my heart for the values that God wants to deposit. God may highlight many things but I like to break them up.

We often struggle between navigating two types of values: situational and staple. Our staple values are the ones that are a constant to us. They may include, but are not limited to, things like our relationship with God, long-standing relationships with others, and health and wellness. Then we have situational values that center on what a particular stage of our life requires. College students must value studying if they desire to master the information being presented to them. Once they've completed their education, they're able to release that value.

The simple prayer of "What do You need me to see and who do You need me to be?" has been my way of utilizing my staple value of being aligned with God in every moment with the reality that the moments are always changing and thus what I value may need to change too. I've heard stories of people who lost loved ones but, because they were sensitive in their relationship with God, they sensed before the person was gone that they needed to be more attentive to their relationship with them.

I did a podcast with Tiffany "the Budgetnista" Aliche, whose work I've followed online. Occasionally she has shared glimpses of her personal life as well as her award-winning work. In 2021, she shared the heartbreaking news of her husband's unexpected passing. I didn't know her personally, but I said a prayer and shared my condolences in the

> Allowing yourself the duality of having a heart that's been tattered and a God who is faithful is the only way you can discover the grace to survive difficulty.

comments section as did many of her other supporters.

In 2023, I interviewed her for the *Woman Evolve Podcast,* and she shared with me how the loss of her husband, though devastating, in hindsight was one for which she felt God had prepared her. For the first time in a long time, she felt compelled to slow down the pace of her work to be more present in her life.

I marveled at how her sensitivity before his passing was aiding her as she waded through the absence of his presence. Keeping our heart open even when the pain feels unbearable is how we maintain the sensitivity to what we need to value at any given moment. I know that God wastes nothing, so even when I'm tempted to shut my heart down, I fight to stay open. I don't want to miss out on a divine update of my values that could bring restoration to my soul just because I didn't believe that I could be disappointed and open at the same time.

Allowing yourself the duality of having a heart that's been tattered and a God who is faithful is the only way you can discover the grace to survive difficulty. The first step to forming either set of values is releasing your clench on what you thought had value and opening your heart to the values that God desires you to now have.

If you're learning to open your heart again, I encourage you to take the time to borrow those two questions I shared when you feel like shutting down. When you say those words with faith that God has an answer, you're able to become sensitive to how your environment is working with God to answer your needs.

Once your heart has been opened, the search for the answer can commence. I start my search with Scripture. I've learned so much about how God has reshaped, reframed, or rebuked the values of people through Scripture. I assure you that this didn't happen because I'm a Bible scholar.

On the contrary, I'm just a girl looking for an answer in a Book that has proven to be a salve for generations. There has never been a situation that I've faced that didn't have an answer in Scripture. I grew up in church, and I'll be the first to admit that my Bible must have had melatonin in the pages, because when I would open it up I'd feel my eyes getting heavy and slumber falling on me.

I had to be honest with myself about not knowing where to start with such a big Book. I learned to overcome this hurdle by opening up my Bible and Google at the same time. I'd put in a simple search, like "Scripture about disappointment." Instantly I could choose from pages of Scriptures that spanned the Old and New Testaments. I'd skim through a few until one pricked my heart.

Then I would flip open my Bible and read the whole chapter of whichever scripture made my heart feel a little less achy. Searching for scriptures about courage, worry, doubt, heartbreak, or fear is how I began to tap into how God redirected what a person in a similar situation to mine should value.

What I loved about doing those searches is that most of the scriptures that came up are scriptures about God, Jesus, or the apostles professing what not to do and what to do instead. For instance, when Joshua was leading a generation of people who were finally entering into a territory that was promised, God gave Joshua insight on the ultimate plan He had and how Joshua should position himself for success.

Joshua 1:6–7 says,

Be strong and of good courage, for to this people you shall divide as an inheritance the land which I swore to their fathers to give them. Only be strong and very courageous, that you may observe to do according to all the law which Moses My servant commanded you; do not turn from it to the right hand or to the left, that you may prosper wherever you go.

Right before God gave Joshua this command, He let him know that one season had ended and a new season was beginning. Joshua, who was the assistant to the deceased leader, was now being positioned to take command. In order for him to effectively shift from servant to servant-leader, he would need a new set of situational values.

All we know is that Joshua was a trusted, loyal servant to the previous leader, which means that he must have placed value on serving that leader with intention and dedication. Now that he was leading, God was letting Joshua know that his success as a leader would depend on him being strong.

The Hebrew word for strong is châzaq, *khaw-zak´*, and its primitive root means "to fasten upon; hence, to seize."[3] God was informing Joshua that as a part of his new value system, he could no longer value being an obedient servant but rather a relentless leader who fastened onto the promise that God had given.

Unpacking the book of Joshua reveals that the territory promised to Joshua's people would be contested many times. There were even moments when the people he'd been tasked to lead were frustrated and overwhelmed by the magnitude of their opposition. If Joshua didn't learn how to be a fastener, he could not teach those he was influencing to do the same. Alternatively, if he did not demonstrate strength, his values could have been swayed and he would have surrendered to the whims of the people instead of leading them with confidence.

> What you value determines how you show up, and how you show up determines what doors are open to you.

If you truly believe that God is all-knowing and all-powerful, then when you lean into His vision for your values, you are being positioned for what will grant you access to the version of yourself that has the most power for the task at hand. What you value determines how you show up, and how you show up determines what doors are open to you.

Flip the Switch

MARINATE

What values do you need to possess to have the powerful life you envision?

ACTIVATE

Intentionally plan an activity or conversation that will force you to draw upon the value you desire.

PRAY

God, help me to honor the values that make me a worthy vessel of Your power.

CHAPTER 4

THE ECOSYSTEM OF YOU

ONE WOULD FIND IT STRANGE IF A PERSON MADE THE SAME MEAL every day. Until they looked in the pantry and realized that the person was simply preparing a meal based off the available ingredients. It's like a college student who eats ramen every night; it's not that they don't have a taste for something else, it's that they are incapable of accessing what they actually have an appetite for. If you have ever found yourself hungry for a version of yourself that you can envision but not access, you're not alone.

When you take the time to cultivate the core values that align with the most powerful version of who you are, you are changing your appetite, but when you get ready to live those values out, you have to change what's in your pantry. Otherwise you'll have an appetite for a version of yourself that you're not equipped to produce. You have to do the work of implementing systems that make your core values easily attainable.

You may value self-care, but your programming is not currently set up to allow you to make room for yourself. Instead of breaking out of the system, you might become resentful and frustrated. You may value the connection of friends and family, but the pursuit of stability and success makes it difficult for you to honor those values.

There has been plenty of content that centers around the notion "if a person wanted to, they would." This suggests that if you're more valuable to them than their demanding schedule or pursuit of their goals, they will make time. I believe that this argument holds some truth, but I also know firsthand how challenging it is to channel what you value into your actions. Your systems are wired in your brain, but your core values exist in your heart. Without the proper system in place, what's in our hearts won't show up in our actions.

If one of your core values is empathy, but the moment someone shares their experience with you, you get impatient or think their pain is trivial, it's not that you have the wrong value, the issue lies within the way that you're processing their journey. More than likely, you haven't yet learned how to hold space for experiences that are unfamiliar. What do you need to change about the way that you're currently wired to make sure that empathy is rising to the surface?

Is this a safe space? I'm just going to believe by faith that you said yes. I'll share with you that I was a year or so into my marriage when I realized that I needed to make honesty a part of my core values with my husband. You better not be judging. If you would have asked me whether I was an honest person before this decision, I would have said yes.

I realized though that I had a tendency of avoiding potential conflict or disappointment by keeping my truth to myself or lying by omission. I did not consider this to be dishonesty. I thought I was doing what was necessary to keep the peace. After he called me out a few times I realized that while I wanted to claim honesty as a part of my core values, my actions revealed that what I actually cherished was people pleasing.

If we don't examine the systems we created to survive, they can become viruses that keep us from health. It doesn't happen as much now, but with one click on the wrong website a computer could go from functioning as normal to becoming a headache for its user. In some instances, the effects of the virus are immediately visible. In other instances, it could be days or even weeks before the malware is evident.

I can remember being confused that a song I downloaded from a less than reputable site was the culprit for technical issues weeks later. It wasn't until my computer yielded repeated undesired results that I began to investigate whether a virus was working behind the scenes. The desire to change the results that you're getting in life requires you to do more than refine your values. You must examine your inner systems for potential viruses that sabotage the transformation that you want to experience.

GET UNCOMFORTABLE

Has anyone ever told you to abandon your comfort zone? It sounds good on paper, but there's a reason why we stay nice and cozy in our safe place. It's because we know how everything works there. Your comfort zone was constructed by an architect named *trauma*. The plans for the comfort zone are clear: mitigate any and every possibility for emotional, physical, mental, or spiritual damage by any means necessary. To ask someone to abandon their comfort zone is to request they surrender a sense of safety.

Logically we know that the commitment to living in our comfort zone does not completely eliminate the chances of pain, disappointment, rejection, or vulnerability, but it also does not welcome it with open arms. When our survival instincts became the architect for our comfort zone, they took note of how engaging or avoiding certain topics made us feel safe or alone.

They determined the best path for navigating interpersonal relationship dynamics and built walls where appropriate, sometimes blocking people who could help us in the process. Lastly, survival convinced us that avoiding challenges or opportunities that require vulnerability would give us control and longevity.

When all these elements began to work together, it created the framework of you. In this realm, experiencing rejection, isolation, or unbearable intimacy is decreased significantly because outcomes are predictable. Processes that produce predictable outcomes are also known as systems. When guesswork is taken out of outcomes, we have successfully programmed an existence that we are confident won't harm us. But just because it's not harming us doesn't mean that it's helping us.

Anything that trauma builds has an expiration date. You built a world of safety and predictability based on the dangers that were present then, but it's possible that you're using programming for a circumstance that no longer exists. In trauma therapy, counselors work with individuals who are still enacting the coping mechanisms that helped them to survive their trauma in a world where the threat no longer exists.

I don't want you to be so programmed to survive that you miss out on the update that transforms you into being programmed for power. It's no different than a computer running with an undetected virus. What deposits did your trauma leave behind in its aftermath and how has it deterred you from living with faith and power? If you have found yourself unpleased with your comfort zone and you're wondering how to break free, you shouldn't take a bold, adventurous leap of faith until you've taken the time to understand your programming. Otherwise, you'll take the leap of faith . . . but leap right back into your comfort zone when the outcomes become too unpredictable because you're wired for survival.

There is nothing wrong with having a system. The most efficient computer is able to function healthily because of a system in place. It's not possible to show up in all the ways that you do without a framework that takes into account the limits and boundaries you need to feel stable and productive, and a healthy contributor to your community is not possible without being properly programmed. However, systems that have not been interrogated become viruses that snuff out our fire before it can even blaze. This internal malware spreads inadequacy, fear, doubt, and worry that quenches your potential and blocks your blessings.

Speaking of spreading, I think you should know that the beliefs, perceptions, and relationships that construct our comfort zones don't just appear out of nowhere. The reason those elements are accessible in the first place is because they are readily available in the cultural environments in which we exist. When scanning for potential viruses in your way of being, you can't help but ask: How has my upbringing shaped my programming?

The philosophies, relationships, and communication styles that you possess are the fruit of the environment that shaped you. It's what was within reach when you needed to define love, success, responsibility, and integrity. Underneath every family, culture, place of employment, or friendship is a system of rules that promises safety and defines what's important, appropriate, fair, and valuable, and what's not.

You may have been programmed to fear scarcity, laziness, or lack, but now your body is deteriorating and you're tired before the day begins because you feel guilty when you rest.

Maybe you've been programmed to please others before you consider yourself and now you feel resentful when your needs go unmet. I know people who were programmed to trust no one and to need no one, and now they're unable to experience intimacy in relationships. One of my favorite stories in the Bible is when Jesus was left behind in Jerusalem. His mother, Mary, and earthly father, Joseph, finally found Him after three days, and Jesus' response has always stuck with me.

> And He said to them, "Why did you seek Me? Did you not know that I must be about My Father's business?" But they did not understand the statement which He spoke to them. (Luke 2:49–50)

Jesus was confused that they were expecting human behavior from someone who was programmed for divinity. Mary and Joseph did not just leave Jerusalem with their child; they left with an awareness of how He was wired that would serve them in raising Him. Sometimes the greatest gift you can give the people you're connected to is an insight into how you are programmed.

When my husband and I were first married, I'd become unnecessarily defensive when he asked me, "What were you thinking?" Though his tone did not have any malice, the words struck a nerve. I had been asked this question growing up whenever I made a poor decision, and as a result of me being programmed for shame, when my husband asked me the same question, I could not respond maturely.

I finally let him know that—though I was updating my programming—his question made me instantly feel the shame from making poor decisions in the past. I told him I was working through it because I will not accept any programming that draws me away from the love of God or the love that God has placed in my life. You are not supposed to be governed by your programming; you're supposed to be governing your programming.

I'm praying that as you ingest this message, God would give you the desire to question the way you are programmed. Some of you already know that you've been programmed to play it small for far too long. It's time for you to break covenant with the wiring that has comforted you so that you can receive the update that God went to great lengths to make sure you could receive.

When I was fresh off the heels of a divorce, the idea of marrying again felt preposterous. After I began to heal, I knew that if I remarried, I wanted my future husband and me to share similar philosophies about parenting. As elementary as it sounds, we often see couples asking whether a potential suitor wants to have children when what would be more beneficial is asking how they want to parent those future children. Your parenting philosophies will determine what programming your children will receive.

I spend a lot of time studying human behavior. I've learned so much through reading and listening to thought leaders in that space. Even when I was a young girl, before binge-watching on an app was a thing, I'd watch marathons of a show called *Intervention* for hours.

Though I was still an adolescent at the time I watched the show, I was fascinated by the stories profiled. I think it's because I was trying to understand my inner torment by watching someone else navigate their own. The brave souls in the throes of addiction shared their lives with the world and unknowingly allowed me to experience my first introduction to therapy.

I could always count on a moment when the counselor was able to see beyond their addiction and find the virus that had intercepted their programming and birthed the desire to escape through substance abuse. The person grappling with substance abuse resorted to their narcotic of choice because temporary reprieve was better than no relief at all.

The only thing that mattered to the person on the show was maintaining the euphoric state of oblivion to their pain. That pursuit of this "freedom" blinded them from seeing that they were planting the very pain seeds that initiated their trauma in the lives of others. Their friends and family wanted freedom for them too, but the healthy kind that cannot be easily undone.

I watched as the therapist helped their client expand their perspective from focusing on getting clean or reconnected with life the way they once knew it, to cleaning out the virus that made substance abuse their comfort zone in the first place. Once that work was done, an introduction to the possibility of new ways of functioning could emerge and a power seed could occupy the space a pain seed once called home. Different shows left me with different nuggets, but there was a universal truth that existed in them all: transformation does not come without discomfort, and becoming powerful will be uncomfortable before it becomes liberating.

FIND THE VIRUS

You may be holding yourself accountable for your inability to overcome a particularly burdensome circumstance in your life, but perhaps your time would be better spent understanding the malware that created the circumstance in the first place. Too often we look at the outcomes of our lives at face value. We penalize ourselves for our inability to make tough decisions. The fault is not our own. Underneath the surface of whatever or whomever you're trying to break free from is a virus that has distorted your confidence.

> "And I will put enmity
> Between you and the woman,

And between your seed and her Seed;

He shall bruise your head,

And you shall bruise His heel." (Genesis 3:15–16)

Part of the reason Genesis 3 had generational implications is not just because the man and woman ate from the tree and sin entered the world; it's that sin's entrance also inserted a virus that seeks for you to arrive at a state of shame, humiliation, pain, fear, and rejection. In this system we constantly question God's intentions. It's a system of pain and distrust. A system that made it more difficult than necessary to experience uninhibited connection with God. It is still functioning today because viruses like this are difficult to break. It is so powerful that it doesn't even have to rely on a specific person to stay alive.

When we're proud of the systems, we call them traditions. When we're haunted by them, we call them generational curses. There are systems at play in our world that we'd like to see dismantled, but they seemingly hold more power than we do. That is not by coincidence. There are families that are incapable of demonstrating vulnerability because they're trapped in a framework that can only survive if their strength is defined by suppressing emotions and avoiding tough conversations.

The reality that inner-city families are more prone to illness, food insecurity, and underserved resources in their schools is not coincidence. It is the byproduct, and intent, of the system from which many are determined to escape. Decades-long friendships that center around celebrating milestones and comforting in times of devastation are not something that a group gathers, votes on, and then implements. It's a system that starts off new and foreign and then becomes the norm.

Systems are meant to take the work out of thinking about what to do. An autopilot of actions and reactions that becomes second nature. Financial responsibility and generational wealth do not just occur. Seeds are introduced that make them possible. In an organization it's imperative for a system to exist, otherwise things would be chaotic. The system determines the flow of communication and the journey from ideation to actualization.

There does come a time, though, when even the most successful organization must be willing to reevaluate the system if they desire to maintain a healthy and productive work environment. Some organizations falsely believe that if they're still able to produce the same outcomes over and over that everything is healthy; but you can't just look at where you finish to determine health.

The folks at Blockbuster were probably efficiently navigating the system that made them a staple in weekend plans across America. Until they weren't. The age-old adage "If nothing changes, then nothing changes" will eventually confront the undeniable truth that everything is always changing.

You must be willing to actively consider whether your system is outdated for where you're headed and whether your environment is nimble enough to withstand the discomfort of your introducing a new system. There's an epiphany that happens every few years in parenting when a child's development alerts the parent that the child no longer needs from them what they once did. From there, a new system must emerge.

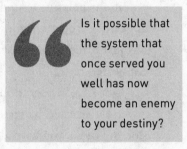

Is it possible that the system that once served you well has now become an enemy to your destiny?

You could be frustrated because yesterday's system has become today's restriction. What if the systems we once needed are the systems that are now oppressing? Is it possible that the system that once served you well has now become an enemy to your destiny?

SAME OLD SYSTEM

I want to spend some time talking about the systems you're navigating in your environment. These are the systems that are active in your intimate relationships, familial dynamics, work, and surface-level social environments. Before we get into that, however, I'd like to explore the internal systems of your heart, mind, and soul. Your internal system will help you understand the role you play in those external systems.

Think of it like an ecosystem. Within one ecosystem there are several systems functioning at once. The simplest definition of an *ecosystem* I could find is "a community or group of living organisms that live in and interact with each other in a specific environment."[4]

The ocean is a great example of an ecosystem. Within the ocean there are thousands of species of fish and vegetation that have systems in place for their survival. The water itself is functioning with its own system of circulation. All of these systems are working in tandem with one large ecosystem. One of these systems ceasing to function properly affects the larger ecosystem as a whole.

The recognition of how our individuality interconnects with the ecosystems of our families, friends, communities, and professional ambitions helps us to understand why staying in our comfort zone is so appealing. You are right to assume that if you were to change, it would not just affect you but would change the ecosystem in which you are connected.

Out of consideration for the people who you presume would be adversely affected by your changing, you have stayed the same. In considering them, you have alienated you. This is not their fault. This is your opportunity to examine the system that has made it easier to disappoint yourself rather than others.

I don't use the word *disappoint* for dramatic flair. You may not consider it disappointment because you received some satisfaction in appeasing those around you, but the etymology of *disappoint* means to "deprive of position."[5] When you deprive yourself of a position of honesty and authenticity, you rob yourself of freedom. Generally it's not a conscious decision. It's one made subconsciously because your internal system values acceptance over rejection. You haven't yet learned that disagreement does not always equate to abandonment.

I am going to mind your business by sharing mine, since no one likes it when a finger is pointed in their direction. We've already covered my marination-before-activation system, but that focuses more on how I introduce positive change in my life. This time I'll be more vulnerable and explain the system that leaves me crippled instead of empowered.

This is a system that renders me stagnant, silent, and hidden. The foundation for this system was first laid culturally where it was better for a child to be seen and not heard. This is not an uncommon system that lays the foundation for adult-child interaction in communities like mine. Ironically, many children who engaged and complied with this system struggled to learn, even as adults, when or how to speak up without being deflated.

As the busy schedule of my parents' lifestyle increased an unspoken paradigm emerged that frustration, confusion, and isolation would be more helpful if kept to myself, and this system grew stronger and more powerful over time. I became a master at navigating things alone. The final cog that transitioned my system from being temporary to semi-permanent was my teenage pregnancy.

As a result, I wrestle with disrupting the virus of silence when I need to speak up or defend myself. When I make mistakes, I'd rather hide than own my need to grow and do better. I find myself choosing to not push the envelope or dissent from what's commonly being accepted out of fear that I'll experience abandonment. I've done the work to become aware when that system is sending me into a downward spiral.

It's important to understand the system that seduces you to power down when you should be turning up. Being armed with this knowledge allows you to better recognize what you're up against when you set out to overpower what has been obstructing you from moving with confidence. It's difficult to overpower an enemy you don't understand. Take the time to think of experiences that leave you feeling the same way consistently.

DIVE INTO YOU

Remember when I told you that you are in the way of you? Your inability to see the systems that are active in your life has limited your ability to experience lasting victory. Let's open your eyes and start searching for those systems, shall we?

I find it easier to work backward. Consider the recurring moments throughout your day when you feel your power is being zapped. The people, city, and environment may change, but your feeling powerless as an end result does not.

Maybe you commit to introducing a new habit into your schedule, but the moment that you get stressed, you abandon the new habit and fall back into negative behavior. Maybe it's not that you have poor willpower, but rather that you have a system of stress in your life that prohibits you from achieving your desired goal.

Have you ever set out to begin creating social media content, but the moment it was time for you to press record, you couldn't bring yourself to step into the moment? Maybe you actually manage to create the content, but the idea of sharing it makes you send it to the archives before it can even be published. What about attempting to have a difficult conversation about your changing needs with someone you hold near? Do you clear your throat to speak up, and then make an excuse to avoid going deep?

Those are some examples I hear often, but if they aren't striking anything for you, then let's try another angle. If it's too difficult to understand your own system, zoom out of the picture and consider the system of your family. How do they communicate disappointment? How is anger expressed? What are the expectations on work ethic? Financial responsibility?

If you have not made a conscious effort to undo the negative systems that shaped you, then the systems that exist in your family are likely showing up in your life. If you have made a decision to do things differently and still can't define your system, I'll pose one simple question to you: What do you intentionally do differently to ensure that you do not repeat what you experienced? Somewhere in there lies your system.

Imagine with me that this system of yours is a printer that marks each sheet that comes out of the machine with odd ink marks. No matter what you print, the same marks appear on the paper. Eventually, you'd open up the printer to try to figure out what's happening inside the machine.

Upon opening the door of the printer you'd see how many parts are working together to print your one sheet. The ink cartridges, printhead, adjuster lever, control panel, edge guides, and more all work together in a system. You may not know how the system works chronologically, but that doesn't keep you from examining what each part does.

If your life is constantly marked with the same outcomes, then the only way to find out what's going on is to open up and see how you're receiving, processing, and responding to the demands of your life. We're going to open you up like a printer so that we can see exactly how many things are working to create the finished product of you. Ever the great friend, I'll go first.

I'm always coming up with new ideas. Some ideas I store for another time, and others I feel are deeply necessary now for the people I get to serve. I'll admit that God never shows me the process of making the idea a reality. Usually I'm lured in by the potential for impact and begin to work to execute it.

I've noticed that when it's something I can do on my own, I feel a sense of safety and security. I know that I won't judge myself if I make a mistake or do something silly. Collaboration makes me nervous because I'm afraid that other people will evaluate my effort and deem it inadequate. The vulnerability required with collaboration is why many people stifle their potential. Nothing truly meaningful can happen without collaboration.

When it's time for me to share an idea with family, friends, or team members, or even through a sermon, I have to be intentional about disrupting the pattern that leaves me feeling like I'd rather be hidden than take up space. Here's my pattern: I start off excited about the idea. I allow my curiosity to run wild through research. Once immersed in the information, I feel relieved that I have a proper execution strategy for the idea.

The moment I know that I can no longer keep the idea as my little secret, doubt enters the group chat. I begin to worry that the reception of my creativity and revelation by another person will threaten my already fragile esteem. I undermine the effort of my due diligence by second-guessing everything.

I forge ahead and release it anyway, though, because I don't know how to suppress a concept that I believe came from God. Sometimes

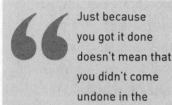

Just because you got it done doesn't mean that you didn't come undone in the process.

that idea is met with minimal to no criticism at all. No matter how well it turns out, I find myself cringing at what could have been better instead of resting in the gratitude of what went well. Most people applaud the results of someone's work, but while they're clapping, the person's nerves and anxiety are attacking.

Isn't it crazy how productivity is not a reflection of a healthy system? Just because you got it done doesn't mean that you didn't come undone in the process. Some people have to work hard to even get started on an idea. That's not where I have to work. My team often remarks about how there's no such thing as me dipping my toe in the water. When I am in, I'm all in. That's probably because I spent so much time thinking it through that I'm ready to run with something they're just wrapping their minds around.

What I do have to work on, though, is reclaiming the confidence connected to what God has given me from the opinions of others so that I can experience the affirmation, validation, and correction that can come only from my personal relationship with God. If I'm rested and my life feels balanced, I'm able to catch myself before I slip into the cycle that leaves me feeling raggedy. That doesn't happen nearly as often as the moments when I'm overwhelmed and running on fumes. During those times I've found myself in the familiar rhythm before I can even help it.

When that occurs, it takes me some time, but eventually I realize that I'm trapped in that same old system that always leaves me feeling inadequate. I stay in that second-guessing stage for far longer than I'd like to admit, because I am still undoing a toxic belief that causes me to feel more safety in being devalued than standing up to the perceived demand that comes with being loved and honored.

If you're going to move in power, it will disrupt the ecosystem of your world, but it does not have to destroy it. A healthy disruption can create more intimacy and trust than staying in the status quo. My intent is not to send you through your world burning down the ecosystem you love and cherish. I am asking you to trust that the environment assigned to bring out your destiny cannot function with a diminished expression of who you are.

I'll be honest and admit that a more expanded you will rub some people the wrong way, but there's a possibility that the rubbing is actually massaging their ability to accommodate you. May God grant you the wisdom to be patient with those who need time to adjust and to distance yourself from those who will destroy your growth. Taking the time to consider yourself is not betrayal, nor is it selfishness.

If you don't understand how you work, you can't target where you need to grow, nor can you effectively communicate to people how they can grow and serve you while you develop. Like a woman who has finally decided what she wants to eat, there are few things more empowering than being able to identify and qualify the systems that are running your life.

Flip the Switch

MARINATE

Draw a diagram of how many systems are at play in the ecosystem of you.

ACTIVATE

Identify a system that you desire to change and the role you play in the system. Communicate one small change you'd like to introduce.

PRAY

God, help me to see how I can be a vessel of righteous transformation for my ecosystem.

CHAPTER 5

BELIEVE DIFFERENTLY

THE SYSTEMS THAT LEAVE YOU STAGNANT AND ASHAMED ARE REN-dered powerless only when a stronger, more powerful belief is introduced. That new belief introduces an opportunity for a healthier, more powerful system to emerge. Failure to take advantage of that opportunity occurs because our new belief must compete with our old system.

God loves me whether I am in a relationship or not. God loves me whether I am successful professionally or not. God loves me whether other people like me or not. These statements are opportunities to believe differently, but until our choices reflect what we believe, we will not experience change.

The belief that I am loved, valued, and worthy of maximizing my life is not one that I grasped with ease. It is a truth that required me to see beyond what I think about my messy insides and to dare to believe that where I see mess, God sees material. Romans 8:28 says, "And we know that all things work together for good to those who love God, to those who are the called according to His purpose."

It's a powerful scripture that has so much meat, but the word that stands out the most to me is *know*. Too many times we quote this scripture, replacing the word *know* with *think*, *wish*, or *hope*. There's something to be said about being in relationship with God long enough that you move from the space of uncertainty about how things work together to a place of knowing.

I have learned that when God causes all things to work together, it's because God is so holy that even the messes I make along the way in the pursuit of His purpose cannot contaminate His holiness. That's not just my truth either. It's yours too. When I fall into the trap of inadequacy because of my negative belief system, I have to remind myself that God did not run out of grace when I messed up. When I trust that I am loved beyond measure, it breaks me out of the system that cripples me. There is a power waiting to be released in you that is rooted in the knowledge that you are inescapably loved, valued, seen, and adored.

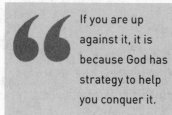

If you are up against it, it is because God has strategy to help you conquer it.

If you are able to grasp this as truth, it will grant you the courage to change your mind about who you think you have to be in order to be palatable. Even more powerful is that it will change what you believe is possible. You will have to learn to confront the ugly strongholds of your systems with the knowledge that God's not finished with the masterpiece of you. If you are up against it, it is because God has strategy to help you conquer it.

I want you to start defining the parts of your systems that make you who you are. This will require some introspection, so I'll guide you through it. I want you to consider a most recent outcome, whether it was the outcome you desired or one that left you feeling disappointed. Then ask yourself what attributes you possess that directly contributed to the way things play out.

This is when it gets easy to begin listing negative qualities. Try not to focus exclusively on the ingredients that are frustrating, like ignoring red flags. There are some parts of your system that you should be proud of too. Besides, this is about building you up, not beating you up. Here are just a few to help get you started:

Initiative

Focus

Pursuing perfectionism

Determination
Doubt
Stubbornness
Fear of isolation
Discipline
Anxiousness

In what sequence did these things come to the surface? If you take the time to look at the stages you go through when meeting new people or starting a new project, you'll begin to see some of the mechanics of your system that have played a role in your being successful, stuck, or somewhere in between. What belief fueled positive outcomes? Which ones wore you down? Taking the time to identify the ingredient that sabotages your outcome is how we begin to petition God for a new way of believing. I'm adding my faith to yours with this quick prayer:

God, please help my reader to believe what You believe and to rebuke what has not come from You.

Until you decide that you do not deserve the debilitating results that your system constantly produces, you cannot break out of your system. And you can't break out of your system if you don't acknowledge where you keep getting stuck. Advocates for criminal justice reform are engaged in the work of dismantling a legal framework that has negatively affected the future of individuals because they believe those individuals deserve better results than what the system provides.

Those who've dedicated their lives to serving individuals in the legal system understand that each case that is revisited sets a new precedent, and with a new precedent, power moves away from endless oppression to a reason for optimism.

Every time you make a choice opposite of what your negative systems dictate, you are serving notice to them that they no longer have power. If you want to know whether your system is healthy, you've got to look at the outcome you consistently produce. Even if the outcome is not what you desire, it can help you to better understand what system may be at play in your life.

I want to broaden your perspective on what you need at this stage of your life. You don't just need a different outcome. You need new convictions. A system that is rooted in love, compassion, worthiness, and the pursuit of heaven touching Earth through you. I'll be honest and let you know that heaven doesn't touch Earth through anyone who hasn't first faced off with hell.

The worst thing you can do when you've gone through hell and back is to repeat the same cycles and habits that bought the ticket to struggle in the first place. There is an authority that comes with surviving that must be enacted so that you no longer live trapped.

The old system doesn't relent because you wake up one day and say the season is over. No, you get a revelation and when that revelation becomes consistent with your declaration and presentation, you will experience transformation. It's beyond being viewed differently because you put on a power suit so that others can treat you with esteem. Real transformation is when what's taken place on the inside of you becomes so evident that the external *must* adjust.

The negative thought process that has left you feeling like a shell of who you think you have the potential to become is operating as designed. It's the same old system that started in the garden. It's the same lies I've had to face and likely the ones that have run rampant in your family.

The template for that system was formed in darkness and seared as an imprint on humanity the moment Adam ate from the tree, but it cannot have your future. It cannot have your community. It cannot have your children. The system has to end with you.

Since the system is functioning as designed, that means you have to get out of line. You must be willing to break free from the system that is trying to break you. If you don't break free from the system, you will never experience the power that is available to you. I know firsthand how difficult it is to break free. I also know the joy that awaits on the other side of freedom.

Soon you will understand that the system wanted you to believe it was more powerful than you could ever be. The system is wrong.

ON THE ALTAR

The Bible is broken up into two sections: the Old and New Testaments. The Old Testament tells the story of creation and follows God's relationship with His chosen people, the Jews. It also foreshadows the coming of the Anointed One, Christ, who would be their ultimate deliverer. The New Testament tells the story of the life and ministry of Jesus Christ, the Anointed One.

While some Jews did believe that Jesus was the Christ, many did not. Part of the reason that many did not believe that He was the promised Messiah was that Jesus did not follow the rules of the Old Testament system. There were certain customs that were to be followed that Jesus frequently violated.

It's important to note that Jesus did not build His ministry on breaking rules and ruffling feathers. I often hear people speak of Jesus as if His whole mission was to rebel against tradition. This could not be further from the truth. Jesus' mission was to restore creation with its Creator, God, by confronting and removing the generational curses of sin that divided us from God the moment that Adam ate from the forbidden tree.

For Jesus, the mission was worth defying the system. You can't withstand the consequences of defying a system without a mission that is more powerful than the

> " For Jesus, the mission was worth defying the system.

possibility of retaliation. I'm reminded of the story of Esther in the Old Testament. She was a beautiful young woman who had found a way to survive by denying her heritage as a Jew. Even when she was chosen to be the concubine of the Persian king, she maintained her disguise.

It wasn't until she was made aware of the persecution of her people that she had some tough decisions to make. What I like about the story of Esther is that she did not immediately grab her cape and go running in the direction of destruction. She had legitimate concerns about the consequences of revealing her identity.

Sure, she'd found a way of existing that required her to not be authentic, but at least pretending promised her a sense of safety. Once Esther took the time to weigh her options, she chose to break out of the system that had offered her peace and to align with the path that would require her to stand on her truth. A study of the book reveals that Esther was not God's only option for liberation, but she was her family's only option.

> And Mordecai told them to answer Esther: "Do not think in your heart that you will escape in the king's palace any more than all the other Jews. For if you remain completely silent at this time, relief and deliverance will arise for the Jews from another place, but you and your father's house will perish. Yet who knows whether you have come to the kingdom for such a time as this?"
>
> Then Esther told them to reply to Mordecai: "Go, gather all the Jews who are present in Shushan, and fast for me; neither eat nor drink for three days, night or day. My maids and I will fast likewise. And so I will go to the king, which is against the law; and if I perish, I perish!" (Esther 4:13–16)

God could find someone else to stand up to the persecution of the Jews, but Esther's compliance with inauthenticity would negatively affect her family. In the end, Esther chose power over the illusion of peace and became a force. You're going to have to do the same. I need you to start questioning whether you've chosen an illusion of peace that requires you to stifle your authenticity.

Esther was informed that her illusion had an expiration date and she could wait for it to all come apart or she could dare to beat it to the punch. God can't infuse strength into anything built on a lie. It's only in the dismantling that we are able to build our lives again with the type of structural integrity that transforms things for our entire community.

There's no better example than Esther to drive this point home because a choice she made to guard herself would have to be sacrificed if she was willing to choose establishing over protection. You can build the walls to protect yourself, or you can trust that God has placed a force field around you. Can you imagine how empowered Esther was when she was able to maintain the life she loved and hang on to her truth at the same time? She thought it was either-or, but God placed her in a position to see that it was both-and.

You don't have to choose between being a strong friend and a delicate lover. You don't have to pick whether you'll shatter ceilings or make homemade breads. You can be the life of the party and a pillar of wisdom. You don't have to relegate power to one expression while diminishing the fullness of your identity. Esther was the queen of Persia and a Jew. Until those truths learned to coexist, liberation for herself and her community would stay out of reach. She unlocked power, changed mentalities, and learned something about herself when she broke covenant with comfort.

Now, that's the kind of power moves I want to experience. I don't want the kind of power that comes from closing a deal, getting a man, building a business, or becoming a brand. Those things can be there one day and gone another. That kind of strength offers only fleeting enjoyment, but it does not radically change you from the inside out. There is a power that is so potent that it radically changes your life.

In Luke 8, Jesus was on the hunt because it was important that a certain woman understand that the power she received didn't happen when she reached out and grabbed His hem. After the woman realized that she could no longer stay hidden and confessed that it was she who touched His hem, Jesus said to her, "Your faith has made you well. Go in peace" (v. 48).

This was not a standard salutation but a revelation for the woman to take with her as she discovered a new life that was not restricted by the dysfunction of her old system. Jesus wanted her to know it wasn't the touch that made the difference; it was her faith. The fact that Jesus highlighted this to the woman is important because it gives us insight into how to defeat the systems in our lives that are causing us issues.

So often we wonder, *What do I need to do to stop the cycle?* Maybe instead what we need to be asking is, *What do I need to believe?* Or even more powerful, *What belief do I need to release?* I want you to build an altar for the belief system that you have uncovered while reading this chapter.

An altar is a sacred structure where gifts or sacrifices are made to God. If you're like me, you want to give God something that feels like a worthy accolade adorned with the accoutrements of success meaningful to our culture. God doesn't care about those things. What God wants instead is for us to give up the belief that keeps us from true relationship with Him.

If you believe that you are too damaged and broken, accomplished and successful, or average and ordinary to be treasured by God, you are wrong. God doesn't want you to just lay down the belief system that no longer serves you. But like any good altar moment, God wants to give you an exchange when you lay down your limiting belief. It is time to have a funeral for who you used to be.

God wants to reveal to you the ways that His power can show up for you and through you. The cracks that make you feel fragile and powerless are the places where the power of God can take up residency and begin to dwell within you. Jesus broke the rules of the system that oppressed them so that you can do it now.

CONNECT AND CULTIVATE

My goal is for you to move from a mindset of self-sabotage to system-sabotage. As you dissect your unhealthy patterns and begin to understand exactly where you continue to get stuck, the next move will be for you to resist the bad seeds. It is only through faith that the mission of breaking out is possible. Faith is not just what you believe but also who you believe.

Coming into agreement with your system of oppression is choosing

to live, sleep, and partner with the enemy of
your destiny. Cultivating the faith necessary to
break free from what holds you back requires
you to have a deeper faith that can be experienced only through relationship with God.

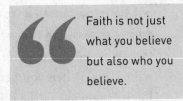

Faith is not just
what you believe
but also who you
believe.

Everyone has their own path to understanding who God is and cultivating that relationship with His Spirit. When you've been hurt by or
are leery of church, it's difficult to untangle the connection between God
and people. I went through this. I assumed that disappointing people was
the same as disappointing God.

I thought that after making a mistake and experiencing disconnection from people is what God would do too. My faith was hijacked and
contaminated by my interaction with people. The reclamation of my
sacred relationship with God has been the thing I am most proud of
accomplishing.

Just in case you're in that place or have found yourself growing stale
in your practice, I want to share my process with you. The beginning
of my relationship with God started with desire. I had to admit that I
desired to truly have my own intimate knowledge of God's presence in
my life. My heart longed to experience the overwhelming and undeniable
presence of the all-knowing, all-powerful God. You cannot be filled if
you don't have hunger.

I grew up in church and I watched and listened while many seemed
to experience radical encounters. Meanwhile I was twiddling my thumbs.
I felt with certainty that there was something wrong with me. I would
recite the salvation prayer at the end of every sermon in hopes that even
though I didn't experience what was happening in the room, at least I'd
accepted Jesus into my life.

At that time, I wasn't hungry. I was just curious. It wasn't until my
prayers reflected my desperation that I began to experience God's presence. God, if You're still . . . was how most of my prayers began. *If You're
still listening . . . willing to give me another chance . . . good . . . here . . . and
so on, then please reveal Yourself to me.*

It's important that we don't make a habit of buttoning up our prayers with a request for things. Instead, wanting to get to know God apart from what God can do for you is the only way to truly be in relationship with Him. When you get to a place where you know God even when life isn't moving in the direction that you anticipated, you don't charge it to God's character, because you know God too well to think He'd do anything to hurt you.

If you've fallen into thinking that God has bad intentions or no intentions for you, I want to assuage your doubts. It could not be further from the truth. Every single thing that God has created, down to those pesky mosquitoes, serves a purpose and adds value to creation. The flies we swat away and the bees we run from are all on assignment.

Why would God get to you and decide to be random? Chile, God is neither bored nor random. There's a role for you to play in this world, and only God can lead you to understanding that role. As you hunger for God to reveal Himself, you must also pray that God would make your heart sensitive to when you're experiencing His presence.

It's not enough to ask God to show up if you're not going to look for where He could be. Finding God in your busy world is like playing a game of *Where's Waldo?* I'm going to be honest and let you know that finding God is not as simple as waiting for a big booming voice to interrupt your day and make His location obvious.

No, instead you have to intentionally set aside time, focus, and energy to search for God throughout your day. You'll know you experienced God's presence when you understand the character of God. The character of God is why Scripture is so valuable. It teaches you what to look for.

You'll begin to see that a stranger on the street was not just kind to you for no reason, but that God used them to reveal Himself to you. Maybe there's a message that comes your way. The person who delivered it may have a gift, but the transformation you experience is not by happenstance. That person has allowed God to work through them.

Scripture reveals to us that God is a healer, provider, lover, and companion, full of kindness, joy, peace, comfort, and so much more.

When you experience that, it's God's way of winking at you. Those who encountered Jesus were left enamored because, in a world full of hate, distraction, rules, and restrictions, there was someone who took the time to care, heal, refresh, and restore them from the inside out.

It's important to me that you come to a place where you are able to be authentic in your relationship with God so that you can experience His authenticity. I need you to practice the sensitivity of acknowledging God in all your ways. There's no way that we can begin to move in power or that we can trust without God leading the way.

If you're able to experience the connection and conviction of God, you can be trusted with power. You cannot have connection with God without conviction from God. There are probably already a few things you're doing that you know you would not be doing if you were standing at them pearly gates.

You're not alone in those actions. Not every second of my day is heaven-ready either, but it is my goal that, little by little, pieces of me become more and more like Jesus.

Breaking out of your comfort zone is not easy. It feels downright rebellious to be one of the few people in your circle to do things differently. As you begin this journey of walking on water and betraying the toxic system that has become familiar, your relationship with God will be your compass. Let Him push you into the next dimension of your power.

You're going to need that compass, too, because power moves you to places you'd never thought you could go.

Flip the Switch

MARINATE

Choose one of these "more powerful than" statements and place it somewhere you will see it every day:

- I believe that vulnerability is more powerful than silence.
- I believe that hope is more powerful than shame.
- I believe that joy is more powerful than pain.
- I believe that the present is more powerful than the past.
- I believe that dignity is more powerful than acceptance.
- I believe that attempt is more powerful than regret.
- I believe that discipline is more powerful than doubt.
- I believe that humility is more powerful than perfectionism.
- I believe that faith is more powerful than fear.
- I believe that wholeness is more powerful than loneliness.

ACTIVATE

Make a decision about what you believe using this belief statement as fuel for the action you take:

I believe that dignity is more powerful than acceptance, so I am choosing to limit communication with _____.

I believe that vulnerability is more powerful than silence, so I am choosing to inform _____ about _____.

PRAY

God, help me to develop the character to support what I believe.

CHAPTER 6

THE MEASURING STICK

I DON'T THINK THERE'S ANY EXCUSE FOR BRAGGING. IT'S OBNOXIOUS and lacks humility, so it's not a brag when I say, I am the best internet interior designer that you never knew about. I don't like shopping in person. I do everything online. I like to search for exactly what I need without having to peruse the aisles.

Having said that, I must admit that I only became good at it by trial and error. I learned a lot about furniture quality, delivery service, color matching, and following the instructions with precision by making mistakes. The most valuable lesson I learned was to measure things before ordering them.

I know. You're probably thinking, *How did she become the best internet interior designer while not knowing that she needed to measure before buying things?* Well, pride comes before the fall and after the fall comes mastery. After too many accounts for me to list, I learned that making the best use of my time, money, and space needed great intentionality.

It's not that I didn't see the value in measuring before. I just figured that I could eye it and determine whether something would fit. It worked almost all the time, but when it didn't work it was disastrous enough for me to say *never again*. I came to a place where accuracy was more important than expediency.

When we're just in our lives and going about our days, we unwittingly fall into survival mode. Our goal is to simply get through the day as quickly and unscathed as possible. When expediency becomes more important than accurately living according to our values, there will be damage.

When there is no intentional effort made to ensure you're living according to the values you espouse, you will eventually find yourself drifting without an anchor. You're "eyeing" it and you may get it right more times than you get it wrong, but there's also a chance that when you miss, you miss big.

Like the examples of the organizations we discussed earlier, your core values are the measuring stick that determines if you're living up to who you have the ability to be. Your ability to live within those principles determines whether you're living a life of integrity. When you compare the daily choices you make to the measuring stick of your values, you are able to see how you're growing your personal brand.

Too often we are content not living up to our values. We give ourselves so much grace that we are impotent at developing the character and spirituality that allow us to be powerful on the earth. I'm not suggesting that you no longer have compassion for yourself when you miss the mark, but I want your compassion to lead to determination.

Having compassion for when you mess up is only transformational when it leads you to try again. I had to learn this in my relationship with God. I assumed His compassion was reserved for things that happened to me, not things I did to myself. Foolishly, I believed in order to receive compassion from God I needed to be the victim, but the hard truth that no one wants to hear is how God has just as much compassion for the victim as He does the villain.

God understands why we make the choices we make. He knows why we are hurting, upset, disappointed, or needy. He understands why we missed the mark, but His compassion for why we missed doesn't change His desire for us to not miss again.

God is compassionate about what causes us to stumble and is compassionate about us getting back up again. Yes, you should have grace for yourself, but you should be cautious to make sure you don't take advantage of grace. You'll know you're taking advantage of it if you go into situations knowing that you're going to live on the outskirts of your values with the belief that God's love and compassion will meet you in the aftermath of your poor decision-making.

Don't take grace for granted. Let it take you by surprise. Let grace overwhelm you with its faithfulness even when you have been unfaithful. When you take advantage of grace you miss out on the opportunity to have your character developed.

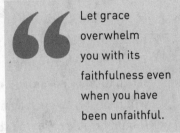

> Let grace overwhelm you with its faithfulness even when you have been unfaithful.

TODAY AFFECTS TOMORROW

Since tomorrow is not promised, how would you want to show up today? What values would you want to be fully aligned with your words and actions? The commitment to relentlessly living a life aligned to your principles is how a person develops integrity. I want you to begin the journey of truly establishing your values and then begin to ask yourself, Did I live according to my values today?

It's important that you make this a part of your daily practice. When marinating on the choices you've made throughout the day and whether they aligned with your values, try to reserve judgment and excuse making. Instead, take into account the different rules you needed to enact today. What different set of values did you have to rotate based on the environment and individuals in front of you? With a simple yes or no, determine if you had a value-aligned day.

Where the answer is *yes*, you should commend yourself. Acknowledge the fact that you were able to honor God's vision on who you were supposed to be in that moment. Where the answer is *no*, ask yourself what made it difficult to live up to your values. Did you get angry? Were you tired? Did you feel shamed? Were you stressed?

It's important to understand what moves you out of the place of living in your values so that a warning flag can go up when you're experiencing those circumstances. When you're feeling unheard, tired, or ashamed, you'll know that more than likely you're also living outside of your values. Unfortunately, I don't always realize I'm living outside of my values until I've snapped at someone or have become irritated by something small.

This is where compassion versus grace becomes important. A mindset that takes advantage of grace may say, "Oh, well. I'm human. This will probably happen again. I do well in all of these other areas, so they should be able to let me slide in this area." The problem with relying on grace is that it disguises pride. When your ego convinces you that living outside of your values is permissible, you miss out on an opportunity for humility to welcome love and compassion from the person most affected by your actions.

Compassion offers a much more honest reckoning. It says, "You have been functioning without being refueled by rest and vision for so long that you can't even see yourself. You should apologize first to yourself for living outside of your values and then to those who've been affected by your inner disconnect." Then plan ways to give your mind, body, and spirit the value recalibration it longs for.

Integrity is not just about honoring the people in your life. It's about honoring yourself too.

FULLY INTEGRATED

I am hoping to instill in you the confidence and power that is only available to someone who has mastered the art of being more accountable to themselves than they are to others. I'm not talking about being selfish. Cultivating a relationship with God, leaning into the values that draw you closer to Him, will allow for the emergence of the most powerful you. When you set out to live according to those values, your life is not centered around living up to other people's expectations, but instead being accountable to who God needs you to be at any given moment.

Sometimes that means that the way people have once engaged with you may have to expand to make room for your new journey. That's okay! God does not call us to live up to values that will alienate us from people He has ordained to be in our lives. The more you choose to be accountable to this new journey, the more you will realize how capable you are of making choices that may disappoint people but elevate you.

Now, before you start cringing at the idea of trampling on people, let me just state that that is not at all what I'm suggesting. There is something powerful about demonstrating empathy when a person has noted a difference in the way they once connected with you. From that place you get to invite them into the reality of how not living up to your values, or not having values at all, was negatively affecting your confidence and relationship with God.

Not every person is trying to hold you back from growth, and some people are actually owed an explanation for how you've changed—heavy on the *some*. These are people who we are walking life out with every day. They are the bonds that have been seemingly healthy as a result of you not living up to your values and may experience some discomfort as you change the way that you've engaged.

The people in your life may have more elasticity than you give them credit for. Give them the chance to meet you where you are instead of overextending to be who they think you are. It is my profound belief that pursuing full integration of our values is the only way that we begin to foster an inner environment that is conducive to pursuing endeavors that require us to trust our insides.

When my therapy journey first began, I spent a lot of time talking about my inner child. I'd never heard of the concept before, but once it was unpacked, it made sense to me that there was an unhealed child inside of me making decisions in my adult life. Part of the work we did was to acknowledge the unhealed areas of my inner child by making adult decisions to express, protect, and trust those wounds.

The goal was not to ignore the moments when I wanted to have a tantrum but rather to do the work of searching for the words to give language to how I was experiencing a person's actions or difficult situation. My therapist labeled this as *integration*. In a similar way, I'm challenging you to experience full integration, but not just of your past self. I want to see you begin to integrate your future self into your present.

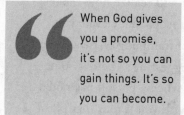

When God gives you a promise, it's not so you can gain things. It's so you can become.

When God gives you a promise, it's not so you can gain things. It's so you can become. There is a way of being that God wants to establish in you. It's not something you will suddenly wake up and have but rather a commitment to enacting the values of that being each day. This is a journey that even Jesus had to walk out on the earth. If Jesus walked it out, you will have to walk it out too. What I love about studying the life of Jesus is not just marveling at the glory of Him as a Savior but also the process He submitted to so His power could be perfected.

Luke tells us that though His divinity was undeniable at birth, He still had to grow in "wisdom, stature, and in favor with God and men" (2:52). Seems odd that Jesus had to grow in favor with God, who sent Him. I always think that Jesus was just being an obedient Son doing what His Father asked, but Jesus had a choice. He did not have to follow the path that God laid out for Him. He could have gotten on Earth and chosen to modify the plan.

Instead, He embarked on a journey of being fully integrated with the human experience without losing focus on His divine mission. That's what I desire for you. I want you to experience the full integration of what it means to be human. Tired, tempted, excited, upset, focused, ambitious, and irritated. Jesus experienced all of those things but still clung to His values of wanting to please His Father in heaven by establishing the kingdom, restoring relationship with Creator and creation, and serving as the gateway that allowed for heaven on Earth.

Believing in Jesus is more than just being someone who attends weekly church services and knows a few scriptures. To believe in Jesus is to recognize that your life has the ability to be a gate for heaven to touch Earth. Pursuing God's vision and value for our lives and living with the intention of channeling that into all we do is how heaven invades Earth through us.

> " It's time for your power to move from pleasing them to pleasing Him so that God can take pleasure in you.

I want you to experience the power not of living to be valued by others but of placing value in your ability to become what God sees. That's what made Jesus powerful. That's what will make you powerful. It's time for your power to move from pleasing them to pleasing Him so that God can take pleasure in you.

Flip the Switch

--------- MARINATE ---------

Think of the moments when someone became an access point for you to experience God's love and grace.

--------- ACTIVATE ---------

Exercise your commitment to new values by doing something unusual for yourself.

    Here are a few ideas to get you started:

        Change your hairstyle.

        Usually casual? Dress up for a change, or vice versa.

        Take a different route home.

        Record/post unusual content on your social media.

        Choose a fresh face over full glam, or vice versa.

--------- PRAY ---------

God, ease my anxiety of leaning into a lifestyle of intentional values and integrity. Help me to not miss the power of partnering with You.

CHAPTER 7

PROBLEM SOLVER

FOR DECADES IT WAS COMMON KNOWLEDGE THAT ONE OF THE MOST expensive depreciating assets that a person could purchase was a vehicle. Anyone from financial experts to expert uncles would caution against investing too much in your car. Then the strangest thing happened in 2020: car production slowed to a halt, and suddenly used cars were appreciating assets. I'm not talking about remodeled classic cars either. Your standard run-of-the-mill vehicles that may have been a headache just a few months prior were now banking serious profit.

It took some time for the world to regain normalcy after 2020, and a couple of years ago I found myself in need of a car right in the middle of the shift back to the way things were. I was in the market for a full-size SUV. Finding a new car was impossible, and the prices for a used car were outrageous! Frustrated by the limited inventory and the obvious leverage of the car dealers, I finally settled, begrudgingly, on paying brand-new prices for a used version of the car I wanted.

I sent my husband the link for the car, fully aware that if there was any wiggle room on the price, he would squeeze it out of the dealership. Let's just say the car salesman must've been made of brick, because my guy was not yielding to the squeeze. I did what any woman who was stuck between a rock-solid car salesman and a strong-willed husband did. I started looking for another car option.

Much to my surprise I found a dealership out of the radius where we lived with a brand-new version of the car that I wanted for less than the price I was going to pay for the used version. The only caveat was that the vehicle was still on the manufacturing line. I called the dealership and learned that they were expecting the car to arrive within the next few weeks. If I was willing to reserve the car and wait, it would be mine.

I went through the process of reserving the car, and even though I had to wait, it was worth it. I knew that I was getting a remarkable deal. Two days later the dealership called and told me that the vehicle had arrived earlier than expected. I could go down to complete the paperwork at my leisure while the car completed its acceptance inspection. I could hardly wait to make my way to the dealership.

I've purchased a new vehicle before, but never one that came straight from the factory the same day. I know that there may not be a huge difference between it coming from the factory versus sitting on the lot for a few days or a couple of months, but in my head it was different. This car had just gotten off the factory line. Before I would even sit in the car it would have gone through months of manufacturing.

While I was thinking of all the ways I needed the additional space for my growing girls, their friends, and activities, the parts of the car were being assembled piece by piece. I was thinking of how I was going to use it; meanwhile steel, rubber, plastic, and aluminum were being twisted and contorted to become what I would drive. Sure, alone those items have some power, but combined those seemingly random pieces would become a machine full of force and power that commanded space on the road.

Interestingly enough, before it could become an agent of power, it had to surrender to a process that would ensure that it had the structural integrity required to maintain the manufacturer's commitment to quality, comfort, and reliability regardless of the hazardous conditions it may face.

Like the vehicle, you are well on your way to becoming an agent of power that represents heaven on earth. You started surrendering to a process long before you picked up this book, but if you've committed to doing this work, then you are moving from the realm of preparation to activation.

Soon you'll begin to experience an alignment that can only occur when God's Word and your life are speaking the same thing. You'll notice that the alignment plugs the holes where power was being drained and releases the clamp where power was being stalled. What happens next is similar to a car coming off the manufacturing line: You're going from preparation mode to utilization mode. You're going from being several parts to a vessel of power.

Many people want to be used by God, but not enough people want to be prepared by God. Jesus did not go from Mary's womb to the stranger's tomb in the same day. Over a course of time He underwent a process that allowed His impact to be undeniable. It's not just that Jesus died on the cross for our sins. It's that Jesus became obedient to a process, even obedient to death, that required thirty years of patience in order to become our Savior.

> Many people want to be used by God, but not enough people want to be prepared by God.

A life spent doing the work so that we can be fit to be used by God is powerful, but our life is not supposed to end in preparation. It would be like renovating and cleaning a home where no one is allowed to live. It's time for you to begin living in this new space. You are moving out of the undercover stage that preparation requires and getting in the action of being used to expand God's reign on the earth.

CAPTURE THE MOMENT

One day the car salesman with the overpriced used car reached out to me about our potential sale. He wanted to let me know that interest in the car was picking up and I was about to miss out on a highly desirable vehicle at a time when finding a car was difficult for everyone. I let him tell his tale, and when he finished, I informed him that I'd actually found the exact same car but brand-new and cheaper.

He hemmed and hawed, then quickly got off the phone. The man had not yet been awakened to what I was beginning to realize. The world had changed again. He no longer had the upper hand. I'm sure he'd had a good run making profit from an unusual time, but the leverage was slipping through his hands. Power had moved again. We can be so busy making the best out of the moment we're in that we miss the moments when what once held power has lost its grasp.

I'll never forget sharing the testimony of my teen pregnancy to a room of people in 2011. I figured once they knew, people would whisper and then scurry away from me the moment I came around. Something quite the opposite occurred instead. Women in their sixties and seventies began approaching me, their hands clasping mine as their eyes peered into my own. Then, in a hushed tone, they made me aware that I wasn't just telling my story; I was telling theirs.

For decades they'd let the power of shame silence them from sharing the fullness of their stories. They were proud of me for doing what they never felt they could. My life became evidence that the power of shame had been extracted from holding a teen mother down and was now being used to set another teen mom free.

When I think about the many exchanges I've had with older women who share similar scars, I wonder whether the times changed naturally or if by telling my truth I somehow forced time to adjust. In other words, are we waiting for our scars to lose influence over us, or are we allowing the scars to hold more power than they deserve?

What if those women who were in their seventies would've decided twenty or even thirty years prior that they were going to dare to embrace God's grace and be made whole? I ponder this because I don't want you to miss the moment when what you once thought held power no longer does. You can do all the internal work in the world, but until you are ready to allow your inner work to be on display, you'll never see how much of a masterpiece you have become.

Confidence is an inside job, but becoming a force is when your confidence gives you the courage to be a solution to what's happening around you. If your confidence is restricted to just making you feel good about yourself, you've stopped short of what it means to truly have confidence. Jesus said, "For I have come down from heaven not to do my will but to do the will of him who sent me" (John 6:38 NIV). Jesus' confidence was rooted not just in what He could do. It was rooted in the knowledge of Him doing the will of the one who sent Him.

> Confidence is an inside job, but becoming a force is when your confidence gives you the courage to be a solution to what's happening around you.

If we make confidence about how we fit in our clothes or how we want others to perceive us, we will miss the moment when confidence has the ability to make us a force that doesn't need validation from possessing a certain image. I want you to have the type of confidence that pushes you into the direction of what you once thought was impossible.

Confidence is not about having the right circumstances. Confidence is trusting that you work wherever God sends you, regardless of your appearance or circumstance. I feel like someone needs to allow this truth to really take up residence in their soul.

There is a confidence that awakens you to the truth that the things you once thought had the power to keep you from doing something for God have now become a pebble you kick to the side so you can finally move with a divine stride.

When you know who you are, you don't allow negativity to hijack your identity. You recognize that what you do is the organic byproduct of who you are. Jesus knew that the miracles He was performing did not require a certain environment. He traveled all throughout His land preaching the gospel and performing miracles.

Jesus trusted that He worked wherever God sent Him. It would be nice if we could stay in the same city with our same people for as long as possible, but sometimes destiny requires that we move into foreign places.

I know that you may want to stay in the same company, city, community, or school. Sometimes we confuse familiarity with confidence and don't want to change because we're afraid that we'll fail. Trust me when I say this: you work wherever God sends you. Are you going to be nervous and afraid? Yup! Are you going to fail? Prolly so.

God did not call you to success without scars. God has called you to the sacred journey of trusting Him through failure and disappointment. Maybe you should stop asking yourself if you can change and still be great and instead begin asking yourself if you can stay the same and still experience God's new mercy.

The old voices of fear and shame that once haunted and taunted you will surrender to the knowledge that you are being made whole. It's like the moment I got to tell the car salesman that he lost his leverage times one thousand! You will be informing your doubt, worry, shame, and fear that their power has moved, and you're determined to move with it.

Inner development lays the foundation for you to become a force. Without inner development you will be nothing more than a blip on the radar of the Enemy. You're easily overpowered at the first sign of opposition. When you reconcile your life you begin to trust God's ability to see you through any trial and gain the resiliency to be patient while God goes ahead of you.

I want to unpack with you the ways that you go from being merely an individual who feels inconsequential to becoming a force that cannot be denied. We've already taken a look at Genesis 1:28, where we unpacked what it meant to be made in God's image.

> God blessed them and said to them, "Be fruitful and increase in number;
> fill the earth and subdue it. Rule over the fish in the sea and the birds in
> the sky and over every living creature that moves on the ground." (NIV)

This verse will be the foundation we use to unpack the original intention for humanity to not just enjoy the world we live in but to transform the world to reflect glory.

When God gave this command, He was not just speaking to a select few who would be granted large platforms, but this is the mandate for every human creation. Our function on the earth is not to be just viewers but to actively engage in such a way that the earth looks different as a result of our presence. It's hard to get to this stage when we're consumed with the work of being delivered from our fears and insecurities, but once you get a taste of partnering with God to make the world better, you can never forget that level of fulfillment.

The partnership takes courage and sometimes it does feel like you're taking a risk, but what's happening inside of you must come out so that the world can experience light where there was once darkness.

ANSWER THE PROBLEM

There is no doubt that we are not short on problems these days. Turning on the news or opening an app will reveal in a heartbeat the depravity of the world. We can allow this to discourage us, or we can see it as a clarion call to engage. Remember that question that I ask God when walking into a new space? "What do You need me to see and who do You need me to be?"

I don't just limit this to the rooms I walk in. I ask this when I see headlines that trouble my soul. I am not just a citizen. I am a solution, and as a solution I feel I have a responsibility to open my heart to the possibility that my gifts and/or talents could be what God wants to use to bring order and restoration where things are in disarray. If you aren't praying about what you're supposed to do within your circle of influence, you are missing out on the opportunity to give your power a target.

There are few things more frustrating than someone who doesn't know what they want to eat but is hungry. I have a seven-year-old who comes into my room often to let me know that she's hungry. I can get caught up listing all the things that are in our pantry only to be met with her saying no over and over again.

One day I told her to stop telling me she's hungry and start telling me what she wants to eat. She may have to go into the kitchen and search the pantry herself. She may need to sit for a minute and tap into her taste buds, but one thing always happens for sure. When she comes back to ask me to remedy her hunger, I know that she's making the best use of my energy.

I want to serve her well, but my energy needs a target. I believe that when we begin to ask God for power to be a solution to specific things that are breaking His heart, we are giving the power He allows us to hold a target that will destroy the works of the Enemy.

This is a much larger prayer than "God, give me the power to lose weight, get rich, or find a partner." I believe that God wants for your life to be happy and your soul to thrive, but part of being in any good relationship is asking the other person what we can do for them. When we think this way, we may realize that God wants to use the jagged edges of our past to help someone nurse their own wounds.

We may begin to pray for power to keep another young person from the clenches of incarceration. We may pray for the power to create a program that eradicates gun violence in our neighborhoods. Young adults may no longer be susceptible to eating disorders or self-harm because God's given us the power to address what's truly leaving them empty.

It's so important that you make your growth about you for a season so that when the time is right, you can spend a lifetime serving those who need your wisdom the most. You need to have a season where you turn your focus inward. When you perform an autopsy on what has died and come back to life inside of you, you're able to better guide others through, or away from, the pitfalls that had you bound.

This is about you becoming an active participant in the change you want to see happen in the world. Jesus could have ascended to heaven after being raised from the dead and said His work was complete, but He visited the disciples because they'd been exposed to too much power to stay where He'd left them. He gave them a charge to spread the power they'd received.

What problem are you constantly seeing, and have you asked God what role you can play in the solution? Is it a problem you see in your family, organization, community, school, or church? Are you waiting on someone to fix something that you're bothered by, or are you willing to risk discomfort to be the solution?

Imagine a house that has been renovated but not lived in. It has undergone a process but has not been put to use. On one hand that's great because the house stays in picture-perfect working condition. To live in the house, you will risk things breaking, burning out, being stained, and being damaged. You cannot avoid the potential power failures that come with being a solution, but with each failure comes an even more powerful realization. Each failure carries with it a lesson that can recharge you for your next attempt.

> " Each failure carries with it a lesson that can recharge you for your next attempt.

God doesn't make mistakes, but in the pursuit of discovering why He created you, you will certainly make mistakes. That's okay. The Holy Spirit is waiting to fill your heart with His wisdom and lessons even in loss. I truly believe that every soul represents a solution waiting to be released in the earth.

Flip the Switch

MARINATE

List the biggest problem you've identified in your community.

ACTIVATE

Explore the perspectives of other people in your community and determine if there's an opportunity for a solution.

PRAY

God, stir up the hunger for resolve in the problems that I see. Send me in the direction of those ready to effect change.

CHAPTER 8

FILL THE EARTH

WHENEVER I HEAR THE CREATION STORY, I ALWAYS THINK THAT WHEN God presented Earth to Adam, He gave him a finished product. The immediate idea of living in the garden of Eden that comes to mind features two people in a perfectly climate-controlled garden where they could easily pick their breakfast from a tree, take a nap, pet some animals, dip in the river, and sunbathe.

Even when we talk about presently suffering through the consequences of their mistake in the garden, we talk about it like they interrupted what would have been a life akin to vacationing and forced us to clock into a life full of labor and hard work.

There's no doubt that their mistake intensified the physical, emotional, and spiritual labor connected to our existence, but when I look at Genesis 1:28 again, what I see is the reality that God always intended for us to spend portions of our life pursuing productivity. When God gave them dominion over the earth, the earth itself was just a seed. They were charged with the responsibility of bringing it to its full potential.

The first thing that God told Adam and Eve after He said to be fruitful and multiply was to fill the earth. Most theologians agree that being fruitful and multiplying is the act of having a family. I believe that this is in part what God meant, but I don't think it was limited to having children for the sake of having children. There are a lot of people creating children, but they are not making them image bearers. God gave them a big responsibility when He told them to be fruitful and multiply.

I believe that God ultimately desired for them to be intentional about multiplying His image on Earth. As we know, that's not just having sex and creating children. That's truly living a life that models what receiving God's love, affirmation, validation, and purposes can look like. It's living a life that is worthy of impartation.

God's original intention was for Earth to take on the attributes of heaven. He gave Adam and Eve a formula for how to make that happen, but sin's entrance built a wall that made Earth become a crockpot of heaven, hell, humanity, fear, decadence, and pain. Now, if I were God, I would've gone about minding my business, like Earth was an ex that missed out on the best thing that could have happened to it. No surprise that God is better than me.

He did not give us what we deserved.

He did not give up on who we could become.

God did not let go of the notion that heaven could still find a home on Earth. He just realized we were going to need some support to get it done. Jesus came to restore the bridge between heaven and Earth.

When Jesus professed that the kingdom of heaven was at hand, He was letting us know that there is no more division between heaven and Earth. Had Adam and Eve not been disobedient in the garden, the kingdom of heaven would have been established through them, fulfilling the original mandate given to them in Genesis.

Even if children are not in the plan for your life, it doesn't mean that you can't be fruitful. You are able to become fruitful by taking the seeds God has placed in you and bringing them to fruition. You multiply when you make sure the fruit of your life doesn't end with you. You're not just a person taking up space on this planet. You are a seed thrower.

Anytime you give your wisdom, serve another person, share a post, or offer a listening ear, you are multiplying God's image on Earth. As if that were not enough responsibility, the next list of tasks God gave would have certainly sealed the deal.

God told His fresh creation that they needed to fill the earth. Now, either God really wanted the earth to be full of people, so He mentioned it three different times: fruitful, multiply, and fill the earth. Or God was not referring exclusively to procreation. God was giving them an insight that only He fully understood.

DON'T LOSE YOUR BASE

As lush and as full as their surroundings may have been, it was only a portion of what's possible in the earth. The garden of Eden was not the only place on Earth. It's just the place that God created to be their home. Genesis 2:8–9 lets us know that the environment God placed them in was to be a place that was beautiful and delicious:

> The Lord God planted a garden eastward in Eden, and there He put the man whom He had formed. And out of the ground the Lord God made every tree grow that is pleasant to the sight and good for food. The tree of life was also in the midst of the garden, and the tree of the knowledge of good and evil.

Later on in verse 15 it says:

> Then the Lord God took the man and put him in the garden of Eden to tend and keep it.

Why would God give them the responsibility of subduing the *earth*, having dominion over the fish of the *sea*, over the birds of the *air*, and over *every living thing* that moves on the earth, then relegate them to staying and tending to a flourishing garden? God knew that their existence would extend beyond their initial territory.

Whether by exploration or being exiled, they would see that the place where they started would not be the place where they landed. I love when a scripture gives us insight into the character of God. Here I learn that you need a solid base before you can reasonably expand.

Far too many people beat themselves up for not being further along in life, but they fail to take into consideration how far they've come considering the instability in their base. If you've gone from sinking foundation to sinking foundation, it can frustrate you and make you believe you're incapable of establishing.

The work that we've done regarding your systems and values is not just a novel idea. I wanted to help you establish a firm foundation so that you can build without fear of irreparable demolition. When Adam and Eve were banished from the garden, they lost life as they'd known it. However, they didn't lose the fundamental base that even when God holds you accountable, He doesn't forsake you or abandon you. That's the only kind of base worth building on over and over.

In my head I imagine that Adam and Eve walked out of the garden, and it was like two people from a ritzy private school being dropped off to record an episode of *Scared Straight*. It immediately became clear that what Adam and Eve were exposed to in the garden was a stark contrast to the reality they were experiencing outside the garden.

They must have had an aha moment when they realized that life outside the garden, though full of creatures and habitats, was also empty. What they'd been exposed to helped them understand the possibilities of what could happen in the uncultivated land where they were banished. Sometimes what you have been exposed to won't make sense until you get to where God is taking you.

Exploring this thought was the first time I realized that as vibrant and collaborative as God's creation was, He still gave Adam and Eve the charge to fill the earth. Everything we hear about Genesis 1 suggests that the earth was set in motion and that all humanity had to do was step into it. However, the command to "fill the earth" offers us a contradictory view. Things can be set in motion and even seemingly full, but still empty.

God let them know in advance to not settle for the systems they saw, and to intentionally seek opportunity to bring into fruition what they didn't see. When I look at the current state of our world, I often wonder how much of it is actually full or if we are watching emptiness in motion.

MORE THAN MEETS THE EYE

I find myself logging off social media just to clear my head because the world is full of so many voices. I turn the TV on to watch something entertaining, and even though there's plenty to watch, everything still looks empty.

I drive through my city and see how quickly things are developing and wonder what will be taking up space where there is vacancy in the next five to ten years. I am constantly having to remind myself that just because the world looks full doesn't mean it's not empty.

I am convinced that when God looks at our world He's not distracted by the standing structures. He's not looking at a Google Maps street view with sidewalks, apartment homes, communities, and structures. God sees the busy souls that are still empty. God sees the bustling cities that are still empty. God sees the full churches with leaders that are still empty.

So how do we fill the earth? We add the substance of our inspired growth and development in bearing God's image into the conversation. I know. It may seem unnecessary to add more noise into an already busy world, but God's given a unique offering that will break through the noise and fill in the emptiness of the person who needs your voice the most.

You can break through the clamoring of your family's culture and your friends' norms. You don't have to wait until you're polished and eloquent before raising your voice in opposition to what's become acceptable. Breaking through the noise begins with occupying the territory where fear, anger, bitterness, ego, and pride have left holes in the confidence and power of your community.

You'd be surprised how much distinction you carry when your gifts and talents are not an imitation of what someone else has said or done. The authentic release of you has undeniable power that can fill the earth.

When you no longer pretend that you aren't who you are, you add value where there was emptiness. Where are the gaps in your community and industry, and how can you utilize who you've become to not just promote self but to fill gaps?

I often marvel at the people who've been able to create resources and communities for others simply by filling a need that no one saw but them. Have you ever heard of Buy Nothing communities? There are more than 7.5 million Buy Nothing community members that span 128,000 communities around the world.

Their primary focus is to "offer people a way to give and receive, share, lend, and express gratitude through a worldwide fight economy network in which the true wealth is the web of connections formed between people."[6] I never noticed that there was an empty space for something like this in the world, but the moment I heard about the community, it instantly made sense.

Of course, we'd all be better if we worked together to fulfill our neighbors' needs, but it requires the ability to gather outside our bubbles and to organize a way for exchange to occur globally. The founders of Buy Nothing accomplished this.

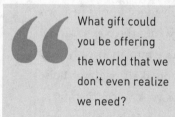

> What gift could you be offering the world that we don't even realize we need?

What gift could you be offering the world that we don't even realize we need? We've got to learn to not be distracted by what looks like fullness so that we don't miss the opportunity to do our part in filling the earth. Let me just say this, before you start minimizing what you carry because you think someone else has already brought it to the table: It doesn't matter how many people are doing the thing that you do. If God has laid it on your heart to do, it's so that you can fill a spot that's empty.

Part of being a solution is searching for the place where you've experienced God's faithfulness and allowing your life to serve as a testimony worth pouring into someone else who is experiencing emptiness. Filling the empty places will look different for everyone. There are likely empty places right in your family, friendships, workplaces, and communities.

It may be as simple as sending a card, making a meal, or creating places for connection in environments that can be large and overwhelming. Think about the ways that you have become full and how you could pour into someone else.

TAKE YOUR REIGN

Adam and Eve would have been so busy being fruitful, multiplying, and filling the earth that completing the full charge in Genesis 1:28 would have been nearly impossible. However, I tried to tell you that God did not intend for them to be down on Earth luxuriating. When I consider the remaining parts of this charge, I realize that effectively completing one part automatically sets the other part in motion. If we follow God's instructions to man and woman in sequence, we will see that filling the earth comes first. Subduing it comes next.

If we go back to the Buy Nothing example, they are certainly filling the earth, but they're also subduing it. According to *Merriam-Webster*, the word *subdue* means to "bring under control especially by an exertion of the will."[7] By filling the empty places they noticed in their community, they also subdued isolation, individualism, and consumerism. This pivot is especially helpful and meaningful to me because it impresses upon me that I don't have to spend time thinking about how I'm going to force something into captivity. If you live with substance, the weight of who you are will bring into captivity anything toxic and unhealthy that is running rampant in your life.

There are so many people today who desire to break generational curses with their lives. They think about the virus constantly and it becomes their primary focus. I'm not sure we spend enough time considering that the generational curse that is emptying generations of God's hope and love for them is available space. If you want to break a generational curse, you need to start thinking about what you're going to use to fill in the place it occupied.

Start living like the space is empty and you're ready to pour a new way of thinking, speaking, and being into its place. You're breaking the generational curse each time you live in opposition to what the curse mandates.

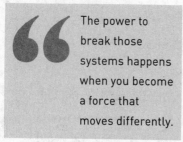

The power to break those systems happens when you become a force that moves differently.

Too often we say we want to break a generational curse, but we're not truly focused on the curse. We're focused on the outcome of the curse. You want to end teen pregnancy, financial insecurity, toxic communication patterns, and unhealthy relationship dynamics. Those are systems that exist in your family, but the power to break those systems happens when you become a force that moves differently.

When you trust that God has anointed your next shift to have enough power to not just move you but everything connected to you, then you will become a force.

Like a kite waiting on a gust of wind, I feel in my spirit that someone needs to know that your community is waiting on your wind to change their path. You may not even be the most qualified in your family to do it. Maybe you're the youngest and the most overlooked, but don't allow your position to make you believe that you don't have what it takes to bring under control what has been wreaking havoc on your family and community.

This latter part of the command stands out to me because it speaks to the mentality that God wanted Adam and Eve to possess and multiply in their sphere of influence. While I want to make a case for a good hamburger right here, I must admit that God was not setting us up to have full tummies when He told us to have dominion over creatures.

I believe God realized that Adam and Eve would experience encounters with species that were different, stronger, and more complex than they may have anticipated. God wanted them to know before they ever saw a lion, tiger, or bear that they had dominion over every living thing that moves on the earth. In other words, God didn't want them to be afraid of beasts.

Few of us are facing off with wildlife in the way that Adam and Eve had to experience, but that doesn't mean that we don't have our fair share of beasts in everyday life. As you position your life to become a force, I will not downplay the reality of beasts that await you. There are long-standing beasts that have ruled in different industries for decades.

From the outside looking in, they look bigger, stronger, and more resourced than you. In 1 John 4, when John wrote to the followers of Jesus, he warned them of the beasts that would await them. He called the beasts false prophets and spoke to the reality of the Antichrist. Then he said something in verse 4 that would serve as a shield for them and can now serve as a shield for you: "You are of God, little children, and have overcome them, because He who is in you is greater than he who is in the world."

When you trust that the greatness of God in you is greater than any beast outside you, you will have dominion without fear. There will be meetings you walk into where you feel nervous and afraid, but remember that you have dominion over whatever nerves and fear are attempting to keep you from filling the earth.

> It's time for the power that's in you to emerge and change what's happening around you.

Any beast that stands in the way of what God wants to do in the earth is not just your enemy. It's God's enemy too. It is not your opposition's responsibility to make room for you. It's your responsibility to become a force that accepts no other option. It's time for the power that's in you to emerge and change what's happening around you.

Flip the Switch

MARINATE

Who is someone you admire for the work they've done in filling the earth with substance?

ACTIVATE

Pinpoint one to two areas where the emptiness truly upsets you. Seek out organizations that may be filling the need that grieves you. Set aside some time or resources to support that vision.

PRAY

God, help me to see the emptiness that is right in front of my face and to aid in that empty place becoming full of Your glory.

CHAPTER 9

OUTSIDE FORCES

WHEN THE DEFINITION OF BEING POWERFUL HAS BEEN REDUCED TO having a combination of financial wealth, great influence, and cultural respect, it's very rare that we are able to recognize how each person we encounter has the ability to be powerful, even if they don't have some combination of the aforementioned characteristics.

It wasn't until people began attaching the term "powerhouse" to my name and messages that I began to question the accessibility and definition of power. I needed to research power because there was nothing in me that felt like I was powerful. I think that's because I thought that being powerful should feel a certain way. I thought being powerful would ease insecurities and release me from nerves and anxiety.

Turns out being powerful doesn't mean that you'll feel like a bigshot boss who takes no prisoners. You'll still have to wrestle with all the emotions that make us question ourselves. Being powerful is giving yourself permission to be honest about your capabilities, desires, needs, and feelings at any given moment and without judgment. It is permission to live authentically so you can show up without preconceived limitations from yourself or others.

Sometimes being powerful is actually saying you're tired, overwhelmed, angry, confused, or stuck. In a world that applauds relentless productivity, sometimes the most powerful thing you can do is rest. You

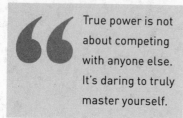

> True power is not about competing with anyone else. It's daring to truly master yourself.

see, if we don't analyze our definition of power with great intention, we will assume a form of pseudo-power that is infused with arrogance and pride. If you only feel powerful when you think you're performing better than someone else, power will always feel like it's slipping through your hands. True power is not about competing with anyone else. It's daring to truly master yourself.

Recently I asked my social media audience when they feel the most powerful. Most of them answered with particular moments that fill their tanks. The answers ranged from getting their hair done to completing tasks, finishing big projects, first waking up in the morning, and oddly enough, when their toes cracked. I definitely didn't dig into that one.

Almost 90 percent of the answers came down to fleeting moments. I could relate. When people started calling me a powerhouse, I wanted to study what was happening to me in the moment I was speaking because I wanted it to translate into everything that I did. I went to my therapist trying to figure out how I can take what's happening in the moment of a message and make it show up when I'm going about my everyday life.

When I'm completely tapped into the zone required for me to overcome my nerves and fears to deliver a message, I feel invincible. There's nothing standing in my way. I'm not self-conscious about anything. I trust fully what God has given me and I will step out of my reserved nature to do whatever it takes for the word God's given me to become flesh.

The moment I finish I feel like the clock has struck midnight and my carriage has turned into a pumpkin. My therapist told me that what I was experiencing was imposter syndrome. She insisted on it, but I could not agree. It's not that I felt like an imposter. I didn't feel like it wasn't me who delivered the message or that I was unworthy of the moment. What I felt was much deeper, like maybe who I am outside of that moment isn't the real me.

The force and power on display when I was preaching was something that I longed to experience in my everyday rhythm. I decided that I was wrestling with something that my therapist could not help me with. This was a conversation between God and me. It didn't take long before I realized that part of the reason I felt a disconnect between the moments when I was speaking and the moments when I was just going about my everyday life is because I thought that power could only have one expression.

Perhaps that's also the reason why most of the people in my social media audience experienced fleeting moments of power too. What if we released our limited perspective on what power is and how it is expressed? Would it allow us to experience the steady flow of power that is ever present?

What if you are your most powerful when you are fully present and engaged in what is happening before you? When we practice being wholly aware, we're able to accurately gauge and assess how to respond and connect with whoever or whatever is in front of us. Have you ever spent time with someone, then reflected on the time and realized that you really didn't feel any more connected to them than you did before?

As a mother I go through the nighttime routine, but then when my husband asks me something like "How do you think the kids are doing?" I barely have an answer. It's not that I wasn't with them, but rather that I was so occupied by checking things off my mom list that I didn't have the chance to truly lay eyes on them. Willing yourself to be present in the moment requires that you shift mentally and emotionally as quickly as your roles do. That's no easy task.

When you are able to do this you'll end up bringing the same power of productivity that makes you great at work into the environment of your home or relationships where patience is more powerful than accomplishment. Because power moves, we must be willing to ask ourselves, What does my being powerful in this particular context look like? Exercising too much of one kind of power in a delicate circumstance can cause damage.

My husband and I wrestle with this quite a bit. We're both visionaries motivating our teams throughout the day and advocating for representation in industries usually off-limits for people of color or people of faith. Sometimes when we're in the thick of tough negotiations, the posture we must take for our mission to be taken seriously in the marketplace is the same posture we bring to who's tucking the kids into bed. Take it from me, the power that worked well when sparring with lawyers will have you clinging to your side of the mattress with your spouse.

The good news is that you don't have to ask that question and act it out at the same time. Let's take a moment and consider all the hats you wear. Child (yes, even as an adult), sibling, friend, partner, coworker, leader, parent, servant . . . First of all, can we take a minute and applaud just how many things you're doing on Earth? There's no wonder you are trying to crack the code for power. Your plate is full.

I don't want to overwhelm you with tackling everything at once, but can you take some time over the next week or so and truly consider each role and the void you're filling? Then, based on the dynamics of your life and the unique needs of the people connected to you, define power in the context of your roles.

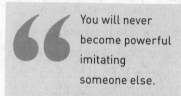

> You will never become powerful imitating someone else.

This is similar to the work we did in living accountable to your values. You owe it to yourself to uniquely define power based on your capacity and unique connections. You cannot expect to be powerful at fulfilling a role that is not natural to who you are. It will exhaust you and render you ineffective at establishing intimacy through authenticity. You will never become powerful imitating someone else.

Other people can inspire you, but they cannot become your template. If you aren't doing the work to study how power is redefined throughout your day, then the things you care the most about will be swept away. You are capable of achieving the fluidity that allows you to honor what matters most to you and the people you are in relationship with at any given moment.

As a wife I can tell you that my being powerful in the context of my husband's unique needs is being honest, affirming, compassionate, and remembering (at least every other week) that a bonnet is not an aphrodisiac. When I'm tired and running on fumes, it's hard for me to tap into the version of me that shimmies her shoulders and comes alive, but when I exercise the power to say "Babe, I need help and rest," I find that my shoulders do indeed remember how to shimmy.

You're not powerful because you do everything without complaining even when you're depleted and overwhelmed. You're powerful when you trust that your world can adjust to your truth, no matter how temporary it is. Just because you know you'll get over it soon doesn't mean that you shouldn't honor that it's affecting you now. You're not any less powerful just because you're bruised.

For one to experience a powerful life they must trust that the steady flow of power is never without reach, and remove the barriers that make us believe that being powerful must always look the same.

OVEREXERTION

I don't think there's an analogy that demonstrates the dynamic flow of power like strength training. When I first began working out with a trainer, I found myself getting winded and feeling exerted in the first set. I chalked it up to me being out of shape. My endurance began to increase, but I felt like I couldn't fully feel the advantage of my muscles getting stronger because the trainer would consistently increase the weight.

Mentally I knew I was getting stronger because I was lifting heavier weights than when I started, but I couldn't actually feel the additional strength in my body. Because he would increase the weight before I could experience the gratification of knowing I'd gotten stronger, I never got a chance to not feel tired so quickly.

Finally one day I asked him why he wouldn't let me just keep lifting the lighter weight for a week, so I wasn't always feeling like I was starting from scratch. He let me know that our training sessions were not going to be the place where my ego could be fed about how much stronger I was getting. It's what I did outside of our sessions that would reveal just how much power I was gaining. He emphasized that as long as I was resting and stretching I would see how my body was transforming. If I didn't feel powerful in my training sessions, I'd have to commit to a routine of resting and stretching that allowed me to see the power I was building to show up in my day-to-day responsibilities.

It dawned on me that the work I was putting in at the gym could not translate into power unless I took the time to stretch, rest, and recover. Isn't it crazy how the thing we think should grant us power doesn't? It's actually the thing that doesn't seem like it matters at all that produces our power. For strength training, it is the resting and stretching.

If I wasn't careful, I'd think that in order to feel more power I'd need to lift more frequently. But power is not about doing more to exert yourself. It is trusting that the moments when you don't feel like you're doing anything powerful at all may be the moments you are growing the most.

God did not stop being all-powerful on the seventh day when He decided to rest. He just understood what would make Him most powerful for that day was not creating, but rather resting. I want to talk about this because I've seen too many fall into the trap of believing that they are only as powerful as their output, but not their input.

There's no use in us talking about you becoming a force if you think the only way you can become a force is by pushing through even when you're hurting, depressed, sad, and overwhelmed. The nature of being a force requires that we truly respect the other forces at play in our lives. You are not an island. Try as hard as you like, but you still will not be able to avoid that you must engage in a whirlwind world and dare to keep your head in the game.

I don't want you to strain yourself trying to exert your power over the forces that are working against your development. There will be moments when you may have to let the other forces win a round so that you can maintain your peace. Please remind me that I said this if you ever catch me engaging in a battle of words with a stranger on social media.

Some of the other forces that we must navigate are negative systems and destructive industries that have been created to promote and protect specific people. They have made it challenging to introduce and innovate because they prefer history and tradition over relevancy and potency.

We're at an interesting stage in our world as we're witnessing a generational shift, whether it's the transition of the royal crown in the United Kingdom or the introduction of new voices in technology, politics, and religion. Bill Gates, once a forerunner, is now a veteran in the technology space, and Mark Zuckerberg has withstood the test of trendiness and become a political, economic, and cultural force to be reckoned with.

The same transition is taking place in communities of faith where fresh ideas for reaching people and extending the reach of the gospel are confronting trusted traditions of the past. As an emerging leader of faith, I'm often asked by my peers how they can navigate the discouragement they feel when their new ideas are met with resistance from an old regime. I always propose that they discover a genuine reverence for the way things were before they suggest what they can become. This rule does not always apply, but for the most part I assume that permission to innovate is earned by respect. If you can respect it they'll let you inspect it.

Chile, as if the outside forces weren't enough, we must then deal with the reality that there are negative forces at play within us. The forces of our anger, insecurity, anxiety, and ambition must be navigated. The only way we can effectively combat the internal and external forces is to resist the inclination to go mind over matter and rest.

In the moments when there is no wind in your sails and you feel that you are all out of ability, that's when you will discover that the most powerful thing you can do is not to lift heavier and for longer periods of time, but to rest your decision-making muscles and stretch your faith. The power of recovery keeps us from making decisions dictated by the pressure of negative forces. It helps us to remember our ultimate goal of alignment with God.

Learning to decipher between when you should be going harder and when you fall back is not easy, but I believe they both have the same starting point. In our relationship with God, we're able to admit that we are in over our heads. In the safety of His counsel we're able to say that we are overwhelmed by our sea of responsibilities.

The Old Testament depicts several encounters that David had with his adversaries. Each time, before he'd face off to engage with them in battle, he'd ask God, "Shall I go up?" He asked this question at times when he was still licking the wounds from the other battle. He brought it up in moments when he was unsure of whether he'd have support from his army.

The same David that trusted a stone and slingshot wanted to make sure that he didn't push through at the expense of being outside of God's covering and support. David understood that his enemies were a respectable opponent and a force in their own right, but so was his God. He didn't want to pursue anything that didn't have God's blessing on it.

A few of us mess up because we ask God whether a certain battle is ours to fight; we've already put on our armor, gathered the troops, and are headed into battle. It's difficult to get a clear answer from God when we're fully invested in the outcome we prefer. A true answer from God about the best expenditure of your power can only be realized from a place of total divestment. I shouldn't have to tell you this because you know better than I do, but we make the worst decisions when we're tired or emotionally/spiritually blinded.

When sizing up all that you're up against, the best decision you can make is no decision at all. Turn all of the energy you're exerting into making a decision and channel it into forcing yourself into a space of rest. Anxiety has been known to push us all to make a decision that tempts to end our misery, but more often than not the decision compounds our misery instead of ending it. *Rest is better than regret.*

A person who is moving with power cannot adequately devise a plan to overthrow their adversary from a place of fear. It means you're allowing fear to move you and not faith. Gone are the days of making a rash decision about your finances, relationships, career, meal, or trips.

Consider asking yourself, What's driving me to make a decision right now, and does it care that my destiny is in the car? I can tell you right now that fear, anxiety, uncertainty, anger, pride, and ego don't care.

You can only trust what's driving your choices when you are able to rest in the reality that God's going to take care of you. I want you to rest in knowing that whatever you're facing can only teach you and not break you.

Early in our marriage my husband introduced me to a friend of his, Phil Munsey, who is always saying, "Your destiny is not going anywhere without you." If nothing is going to pass you by, you can take the time you need to make a decision that has clarity.

Maybe God is using our Enemy's plan to not just change the outcome of one particular situation but rather to change the way we handle every situation. Paul leaned into his awareness of the assignment of our ultimate adversary when he admonished the church at Corinth about forgiveness. He exposed that unforgiveness was an opening that Satan could exploit to create division in what they were attempting to build.

Lest Satan should take advantage of us; for we are not ignorant of his devices. (2 Corinthians 2:11)

I want you to become so aware of the negative systems, fears, adversaries, and insecurities assigned to you in your life that you are able to easily identify when they are seizing your destiny and reclaim your posture of rest. Understanding the reality that there are other dark negative forces at play makes you wise. I know it can be countercultural to get into relationship with your weakness. You can be made to believe that engaging with your flaws will contaminate your power.

The exact opposite is true. The more aware you are of your flaws, the more you have the ability to partner with God in controlling them. Your rest, then, is not in being flawless, but in being completely covered, flaws and all.

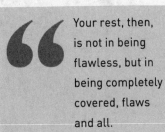

Your rest, then, is not in being flawless, but in being completely covered, flaws and all.

Flip the Switch

---------------------- MARINATE ----------------------

What thoughts go through your head when the pressure and stress of
your life are at an all-time high?

---------------------- ACTIVATE ----------------------

When the pressure is up, intentionally release it by taking time to calm
your nervous system.

---------------------- PRAY ----------------------

*God, help me to invite Your peace into my spirit when my thoughts are being
driven by negative forces.*

CHAPTER 10

THE FORCE IS REAL

THERE'S A SAYING I'VE SEEN THAT'S GONE VIRAL ON SOCIAL MEDIA: "The devil works hard, but God works harder." I like this quote because it is a reminder that when we begin to truly tap into our divine identity of being made in the image of God, our reign will not go uncontested. Isn't it interesting that when the serpent wanted to thwart Adam and Eve from having dominion he did not make them question themselves?

The serpent made them question God.

If the serpent could get them to question God, they would stop seeking to discover how they were made in the image of God. If someone came and threw a can of paint on your mirror, you might find a little corner that is unaffected. But eventually the strain of trying to see through the paint would make you weary. You'd stop looking in the mirror altogether.

If you no longer see God with clear eyes, you can no longer see the potential of who you can become. Jesus came to clean that mirror that keeps you from seeing God, and ultimately yourself, properly. Through His model He demonstrates to us what it means to truly be a human made in the image of God who is walking the earth.

 When you realize your path is clear, the Enemy must work even harder to keep you from turning and allowing the life of Jesus to transform the way you view your life.

When you realize your path is clear, the Enemy must work even harder to keep you from turning and allowing the life of Jesus to transform the way you view your life. You'll notice that the moment you begin to walk in truth and wisdom, it feels like all kinds of distractions are in your way.

You're not going crazy; the force is real. The force is trying to keep you from true relationship with Jesus and from having a heart posture that receives a perfect love that casts out fear. In the moments when you begin to feel the resistance and strain from this real opposition, you have an opportunity to enact a force that has nothing to do with physical practices and everything to do with spiritual awareness.

Prayer and worship are the most powerful forces we have against the demonic forces hoping to stunt our growth. Prayer and worship are how we exercise our authority over evil before we even begin to determine what natural steps we may need to take. David prayed, but then he warred. Once he invoked God's presence, he was ready to assess and utilize the practical resources that were available to him.

Most of us struggle because we don't always know when we should be leaning into the presence of God or creating a strategy for our practical resources. I believe this happens because we are stuck in the rhythm of how we've used our practical resources in the past. There comes a point when the same tools no longer produce the same outcome. You'll find yourself frustrated if you're doing the same thing you've always done but wondering why it no longer works.

Instead of becoming overwhelmed by our lack of ability to push towards our desire, we have to go back to the drawing board to make sure that what we're trying to accomplish has been graced to overcome resistance. I know you're wondering, *How do I do this?* The answer is one you're not going to want to hear, especially if you've been frustrated for a long time and you're ready to finally see change.

Here it is anyway: nothing.

What are the ways that you are actively trying to exert your knowledge, experience, strength, and passion in order to procure a particular outcome? Where have you strained yourself trying to build yourself or others? I'm not asking you to be a quitter forever. I'm asking you to rest for a minute.

If we can trust that rest is not resignation, we can give our most precious resources the time they need to recover and come back stronger, while also giving God the room to restore a vision for our lives that does not center on forcing things to happen but rather on us becoming a force released into the earth.

Resisting the temptation to be the captain of our own ship will require focus, dedication, and trust in God above all. From the place of rest you may recognize where you got off-center. You may realize that when you once started pursuing a goal or creating a project, you were full of faith and power, but the fear of it not happening created desperation.

It is possible that you may need to reclaim your identity from the desired results of a situation. Even when losing people feels like you're losing a piece of yourself, you're still no less of a force because they aren't there. You are not a force because of what you have that people can see on the outside.

THE ULTIMATE FACE-OFF

It has been scientifically proven that there are two types of people in the world. Okay, maybe it's not scientific, but my conversations with people could serve as the foundation for a scientific analysis regarding the types of people who dream. There is one type of person who dreams so often that sometimes going to sleep gives them anxiety. They're afraid that when they close their eyes, a wild ride into their imagination, fears, dreams, and even prolific messages from God awaits them.

Let me testify real quick about how God truly knows who to give certain battles to, because I am not one of those people. If the good Lord doesn't tell me before I drift off to sleep, He's going to have to wait until the alarm or my spirit wakes me up. I definitely fall into the second category, because when I close my eyes I am out for the count. This doesn't mean that when I'm awake that I don't go on wild rides, nor do I escape wrestling with my fears and dreams.

You see, no matter what, we all must face off with the reality of what it means to be human. You being human doesn't make you any less of a force. It just means that preserving the power that makes you a force requires you to have a focus more powerful than your detractors. I almost used the word distraction, but I intentionally said detractors because distractions have become so accepted that we aren't as alarmed as we should be when they arise.

Detractors are agents of your opposition meant to detract your power and render you incapable of clinging to the faith, power, and focus required for your mission. There is no better example of a detractor on a mission than the serpent in the garden of Eden (Genesis 3) and the tempter in the wilderness (Matthew 4). Both of these scenarios, though separated substantially by generations, represent the full-circle moment available to us all.

In these two texts we have a woman who did not know she was a force among forces juxtaposed with Jesus, who was born with the knowledge that He was a force among forces. Going back to Genesis 1:28, God did not make it known that Adam and Eve should beware of forces that may detract them from fulfilling the mission He'd given them.

I've never thought about it before, but why didn't the all-knowing, all-powerful God tell them what to look out for? I know that my thoughts are not His thoughts and my ways are not His ways, but I know from raising children that even when I warn them about something in advance, they don't always take seriously the threat that is before them. There are moments when firsthand experience from less-than-ideal choices grabs your attention more quickly than a warning from God.

Jesus, born into Judaism, would've had full knowledge of the original sin in the garden, as well as His parents' knowledge that His birth would be contested by many. Jesus' life before the moment in the garden was likely steeped with the awareness that there were active forces at play desiring to see His ministry end before it fully began.

His first confrontation with such a force came in the wilderness when the tempter visited him. In analyzing the approach that the serpent took in Genesis versus the approach taken in Matthew, I noticed a pattern worthy of sharing with you. This pattern is essential for you to understand because it will aid you in recognizing the tactics that forces of darkness may wield against you.

I noticed immediately two similarities between the encounters. I've already mentioned one. In neither account did Jesus or the woman volunteer to show off the power they possessed. This perspective is important because too often we fall into the trap of trying to prove the power we possess by actively searching for an opponent. God is giving you power to go and grow, not to conquer and boast.

When power becomes about the list of things we've overcome so that we can receive praise or admiration, then power is about us getting the glory, not God. I fall into this trap of wanting to be acknowledged for the hard work or sacrifice I've put into making something happen. I've come to temper that desire with the reality that if I needed to be acknowledged for doing it then I should not have done it at all.

How many things do you do in your life from a place of wanting to be acknowledged and validated? When I'm running on fumes I want cheerleaders to come out and celebrate that I brushed my teeth in the morning. That is when I know that I've become a machine on autopilot in my world and haven't given myself space to be human.

Then there are moments when I receive a testimony from someone who expresses that my ministry changed their life. They thank me for saying yes to God's will for my life, and I make sure to let them know that the honor is truly mine because I know without a shadow of a doubt that what they're experiencing is not me at all. If they never said thank you and I never got a testimony, I'd still be sharing what God gives me in some capacity, because what I want to hear above anything else is "Well done, good and faithful servant" (Matthew 25:21).

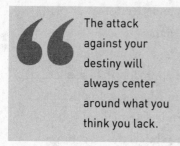

> The attack against your destiny will always center around what you think you lack.

The second similarity I noticed between the wilderness and garden moments is that the Enemy initiated his plan to detract from both of their missions by capitalizing on the deficiency in their appetite. You will never be distracted from your mission by what you already have. The attack against your destiny will always center around what you think you lack.

OVERPOWER YOUR ENEMY

The story ends in disappointment for the woman in the garden, but you may already have a clue that Jesus was victorious, made it out the other side of the wilderness, then launched His ministry. But have you taken the time to truly understand how Jesus overcame the temptations offered by the other force?

One of the things that made faith challenging for me growing up is that it seemed like everything Jesus accomplished on Earth was done with ease. Perhaps it wasn't the way that it was taught; maybe it was just the way I understood His existence.

I think we can spend so much time focused on the divinity of Jesus that we miss out on the opportunity to truly acknowledge His full humanity. When we consider Jesus as a human being similar to ourselves, we'll see that Him laying down His life was not something that was done easily or cavalierly.

Jesus was not an indestructible superhero who went running into burning buildings. Jesus was thoughtful about what actions He would take and when. Jesus' fame grew throughout the territory He traversed, but not because He wanted to make His name great. In fact, He told a man He healed to tell no one of what happened.

When Jesus was in a different garden, Gethsemane, He wanted someone else to bear the sins of the world instead. Though He'd prophesied it to the disciples and knew His ending before it even began, when it was time to step into the moment He was nervous and afraid.

After spending forty days and forty nights in the wilderness with no food, He was actually hungry. After thirty years of being held back, He'd finally been publicly affirmed as God's Son. Perhaps He was genuinely curious about utilizing His power in the earth and exercising it on a frivolous leap. Maybe He wanted to skip the process and just land at the final destination of reigning on the earth.

"If you are the Son of God," he said, "throw yourself down. For it is written: 'He will command his angels concerning you,

and they will lift you up in their hands,

so that you will not strike your foot against a stone.'"

Jesus answered him, "It is also written: 'Do not put the Lord your God to the test.'"

Again, the devil took him to a very high mountain and showed him all the kingdoms of the world and their splendor. "All this I will give you," he said, "if you will bow down and worship me."

Jesus said to him, "Away from me, Satan! For it is written: 'Worship the Lord your God, and serve him only.'" (Matthew 4:6–10 NIV)

The power of the temptation was real, and it was so heavy that it required the Holy Spirit to fall on him *and* forty days and forty nights of fasting and praying. There are going to be moments when the only way you can overcome the forces attempting to derail you is if you insist on a rhythm of connection with God and the Holy Spirit that models what Jesus displayed in the garden.

Jesus recognized that while He may not be able to control what the other forces attempted to throw His way, He could refuse the temptation to abuse His power by putting Satan in his place.

Had Jesus given in to temptation, He would have allowed the power God granted Him to be used to advance the plan of the Enemy. Jesus was the only one who could grant Satan access to His power.

How did He do this, and how can you do the same? Jesus did not just ignore the attacks and wait for them to go away. Jesus fought back by reminding Himself why He could not follow through with the suggestions of the tempter.

Too often we fight back in an effort to control our enemy when in reality the only person we can control is ourselves. There is a difference between telling someone, "Don't talk to me like that," and "When you are able to speak in a way that reflects respect and love, we can resume this conversation."

Now, Chile, don't be using these words if you can't live by them. Seriously, if you're going to be the person of honor and integrity that I know you're called to be, your journey will not go uncontested. There will be many who seek to detract you with temptations or distractions.

You can ask them to no longer show up in a capacity that hinders you, or you can put parameters on your relationship for what you will or will not allow. You know what I love about how Jesus responded to the tempter? He didn't pretend that He wasn't hungry. He didn't immediately tell the tempter to leave Him alone.

> When temptation gets real, don't pretend it has no power. Instead, introduce what has more power.

In an effort to seem unfazed we often lie to cover our weakness instead of redirecting our thoughts towards where our focus should really lie. When temptation gets real, don't pretend it has no power. Instead, introduce what has more power.

You're going to be tempted to connect with that person you know isn't healthy. You're not doing anyone any favors by pretending the temptation isn't real, but the reason you walked away is more powerful than the pull to go backwards.

You may have to audibly remind yourself that financial stability is more powerful than the purchase you're considering. Don't just battle temptation in your head. Use your words to push temptation back. Declaring with a whisper even when you can't say it with a yell is enough to serve notice to hell.

Jesus answered the serpent with the words from His disciplined spirit that would not just edify Himself but also reveal His mindset to the tempter. If I were preaching, I'd probably say something like "I wish I could say this in the way I feel it in my spirit." What I'm trying to express is that instead of talking back to your enemy, allow your spirit to tell your mind what it needs to hear.

Your mind may start to betray you and make you believe that you do not have the ability to move in power on Earth. You may have a history of defeat that has become a weapon against your destiny, but God can use the words that come out of your mouth to push your enemy back.

I'm not just talking about the spiritual forces that we cannot see. When you're tempted to be distracted by gossip, choosing to say instead, "I no longer want to be someone who finds pleasure in tearing someone down" is not just a declaration to your audience. It's a reminder to your spirit of who you are becoming.

How powerful would it be if instead of responding in anger and saying, "If you ever even think of speaking to me like that, I'll become your worst nightmare!" you would say, "I will not allow you to lure me into betraying my peace by acting out of anger." Then clear the room as quickly as possible, because you're not Jesus Jr. and I'd rather your statement be accentuated by your absence than unraveled by your underdevelopment.

Jesus and the tempter had two more points of engagement and contact before the tempter eventually gave up. In each of the accounts Jesus recited what had been written in the sacred book of Judaism.

If you are coming to a place in your journey where the confrontation with other forces is beginning to render you speechless because you don't have the language or knowledge of Scripture to speak that which can edify you, I want you to remember our trick from Google and then dive into a Bible.

The same words that healed, restored, and delivered then have the power to do it now. I've seen it happen in rooms where I ran out of words and notes but began declaring scriptures. Suddenly, heaviness was lifted, healing flooded the room, and breakthrough was tangible.

The reason the tempter had to leave Jesus alone is because there is power in those words. The reason why the woman was rendered ineffective at having dominion over the serpent is because she started reasoning with the very thing she was meant to subdue.

When you don't have the strength to put your enemy in its place, the least you can do is refuse to allow your enemy to pull you out of your position. You have real forces at war over your destiny.

Flip the Switch

When you set out to accomplish tasks throughout the day, take note of the moments when you are detracted from the finish line. God's already taken into account the unavoidable moments you can't control, like family emergencies, car troubles, technology failures, and so on. I don't want you to list these. Instead, I want you to focus on what forces are within your ability to control, like scrolling social media, chowing down on that unhealthy meal, or saying yes to something you know you should have said no to. Don't judge yourself; this is just an opportunity for inventory. Write them down in your phone or journal as soon as you've realized you've been detracted. It's possible that the same thing may detract you more than once in a day. That's okay. This is a safe space.

———————— ACTIVATE ————————

Eliminate your access to one of the things that detracts you for a set amount of time. Unless you're ready to go Jesus-style, it doesn't have to be forty days. It can be one day or seven. The goal is to break your rhythm long enough for you to see how much more productive and focused you can become.

Instead of focusing on the absence of that thing in your world, fill that space with a moment of prayer and connection with God. Even if it's just to express how hard it is to be without that person or thing and to ask for strength, share it with God. Like it was for Jesus, it's important for you to speak what encourages you out loud. Here's a passage that helps me when I'm attempting to elevate my thought life to the level of where my spirit resides.

> *Set your mind on things above, not on things on the earth. For you died, and your life is hidden with Christ in God. When Christ who is our life appears, then you also will appear with Him in glory. (Colossians 3:2–4)*

The old, powerless version of you has died. You're in the awkward stage of figuring out who you are without pretending to be who you aren't. In those moments remember that when you model a life that looks like Jesus, you'll discover the most powerful version of you.

PRAY

God, help me to become more attracted to who I can become with You than I am to the distractions that keep me from becoming better.

CHAPTER 11

LARGER THAN LIFE

HUMANITY HAS A BAD HABIT OF ESTEEMING A PERSON WITH SUCH high regard that we miss out on the reality that they're human, especially in America. We become so mesmerized by their aptitude, talent, or gift that they become larger-than-life icons. It doesn't matter how many times we hear that someone is just like us, we still find ourselves in shock or disbelief when evidence emerges that reveals their normalcy.

The issue with the perpetuation of larger-than-life figures is multilayered, but for the individual on the receiving end of such an iconic perception, maintaining mental and emotional wellness is imperative. If not, they find themselves suffering when new voices and talents emerge and the spotlight begins to shift to someone else.

Of course, the spotlight shifting from one person to another is not limited to prominent figures in media. In more subtle ways we experience this in our social circles as well. The spotlight shifts to a close friend while you're still recovering from a loss. There are moments when you're marveling at your latest victory while your sibling is nursing defeat. There is probably no better example of the way the power of attention, acknowledgment, and celebration moves than in the way it shows up in our relationship circles.

Have you ever seen a movie where you're trying to figure out who the main star is? The opening scene seemingly follows one person until they collide into another person, and then we realize that the first character was just a bridge to the main star. Life can very much so feel this way.

It's as if we're participating in a series of recurring opening scenes where we fluctuate from being the main star to a supporting cast member. I've had many people who've come up to me and stated that they're anxiously waiting for the time when it's "their season." I interpret this to mean that the person is waiting for the moment where they consistently feel like the main character who is experiencing victory and triumph instead of struggling in the background of someone else's story.

Then there are other people who've been the main character for so long that they'd like a break. Sometimes we like to call these people the strong friend. They show up for people so frequently that they've unknowingly become the main character in most people's stories, but we never get to truly understand their desires, needs, pains, and joys.

We cannot reasonably discuss what it means to be a force who experiences outside interference without taking the time to also acknowledge that there's no such thing as a singular force. You are a force among forces. Some of those forces are intent on destruction and detracting you from purpose. Then there are other forces that are clumsily navigating this thing called life and bumping into you along the way.

You have embraced the reality that your power is not just reserved for moments of intense decision-making or that organizing chaos means you're leaving space for rest. When you're functioning with this paradigm that rest and recovery are also a part of being powerful, you will also have to give space for the people in your life to stand tall while you're falling back.

That statement is easy to write but more challenging to implement. I love an individual with relentless determination and commitment to growth, but I also realize that no one is an island and that everyone is navigating their own share of ups and downs. It won't always be your time to shine, and when you are able to move beyond envying that to being grateful for it, you'll notice that it changes everything.

Remember when we talked about how power runs to a light switch?

Though electrical currents flow to the light switch, it doesn't necessarily mean that the light is actually turned on. The power is there, but no one has flipped the switch. When the switch is turned on, the circuit closes and now power is running without interruption to the light.

I'm not 100 percent sure, but I'm willing to bet that whoever invented the light switch did so because they realized that they needed to find a way to be able to choose between power being dormant or active. Otherwise, if left on continuously, they'd end up burning out the light bulb on the receiving end.

I'd like you to consider how you can engage in a power interval lifestyle that trusts when your power is dormant someone else's can be active in a way that preserves you and prepares them. Whew! That sentence was a little too good to me. What if our insistence on being the one who shows up in power all of the time is diminishing ourselves and limiting growth in the people we love?

You were not meant to burn with power every single second of your life. Not even your phone can handle constantly being powered on. Trusting the other forces in your life is one way of being able to experience the much-needed shutdown that every powerful person needs.

> " You were not meant to burn with power every single second of your life.

If I can go even deeper, I'd like to challenge you to not just think about quick vacations. How can team building, retirement, partnerships, friendships, and parenting help you power down? Too often we think about taking breaks as if we're going to hit pause on our lives and then jump right back in with the same cast, plot, and pace as before.

Some people truly believe that they are the only person in their space capable of meeting goals and objectives for those under their sphere of influence. You're probably not one of these people, but believe me, they exist. These people are frustrated from doing things on their own *and* frustrated when people do things because they did not do it the way they would have done it.

Making room for people to show up in their power, even when it's different from your own, is an exercise in releasing control that can strain a muscle. Luckily the name of the muscle that suffers when this occurs is our pride muscle, and more often than not it needs to be strained.

ARRESTING PRIDE

I've often wondered what the difference is between being confident and being prideful. Having unearthed many insecurities, I've found myself pursuing accomplishments that can act as a balm for the areas where I've been wounded. I've thought that even though I may not have excelled in one area, at least I'll have a trophy from another area to make up the difference.

I was wrong. I thought that piling accomplishments over insecurities was like putting concealer over a blemish, but I lived in fear that the concealer would not be enough in certain environments. So I sought out to achieve more and more. When you build a life accumulating things that make you proud of who you are, you never experience true confidence.

False confidence is when you're only as confident as your titles and accomplishments. Subtly, we see pride showing up in our insistence to do things our way. Pride shows up in how we look down on others for the choices and decisions they've made. It's stealthy when it seeps in and it's difficult to arrest, but pride blinds us from being compassionate with ourselves and others.

It's important for us to have real distinction between confidence and pride, because pride is rooted in how much bigger or better you can become than others and, surprisingly, how much bigger and better you can be compared to who you once were. I'm sure you've heard or read someone saying something about the only person they want to be better than is the person they were yesterday. I've probably said it myself.

On the surface this seems empowering and humble, but it doesn't lay a foundation of true confidence. If the only way you can become better is to see who you were yesterday as inadequate, your confidence is constantly being built and then demolished with each dawning of a new day.

I hate to break it to you, but being better than you were yesterday may not be possible. The way life is set up, your yesterday can be peak adulting behavior filled with timeliness, patience, focus, and discipline. Tomorrow you could regress back to who you were five years ago with one phone call. On those days, if you lay your head down in shame, then you know that what you're pursuing is not actually confidence but rather pride.

I recently experienced one of those spontaneous regressions. It happened when I was on a speaking tour. I travel with a team of forty incredible creatives for nightly encounters of worship, word, and connection for modern women of faith. We've done this quite a few times and each tour has challenges, but we rise to the occasion. This time was different. We were going to be in the DC, Maryland, and Virginia area.

A pipe burst at the venue where we were going to host the event and we ended up at a church where my parents have been friends with the leaders for decades. This should have made me feel more confident, but instead I felt more insecure. That's because almost ten years earlier I was a completely different version of myself. I was so engulfed in depression, pain, and shame that rage was the only thing that felt like light at the end of the tunnel.

I was living in the area, and the couple helped me with my two children from time to time. As if that wasn't enough to work through, I learned that another couple who were friends of my parents were going to attend the tour as well. This couple was a safe haven for me in the early days of my teen pregnancy. While they never judged me and always made me feel loved, the emotional intelligence I did not possess then flooded my present. I was drowning in the unexpressed pain of a thirteen-year-old girl.

The day before, I had never been more convinced of my purpose and the impact God was having through my life. All of that disappeared, and just as much as I was the thirty-four-year-old *New York Times* bestselling author and founder of Woman Evolve, I was also the thirteen-year-old pregnant girl and twenty-two-year-old addicted to rage.

I wasn't better than I was yesterday. I was the shattered girl of my youth hoping to reclaim the powerful woman of my present who'd gathered thousands of women to revive their hope in God's plan. I didn't get up that night and pretend my way through. I shared with the room the matrix I was navigating. I think it made them more comfortable sitting in their matrix too. I don't need to feel like a boss on top of the world every day, and neither do you.

You need the days where it feels like you've regressed to remind yourself that your life is not about performance. Finding a way to love every step of your journey while still moving towards progress is the only way to truly arrest pride.

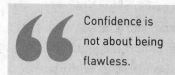

Confidence is not about being flawless.

One of my teachers from afar is Esther Perel, and she offered a quote about esteem that truly stuck with me. "Self-esteem = seeing yourself as a flawed person, and still holding yourself in high regard."[8] If you're only able to hold yourself in high regard when you are blind to your flaws, pride has become the architect of your life. Confidence is not about being flawless.

Arresting pride requires that you intentionally put yourself in situations where you are disengaging from things you know you are great at and supporting someone else's attempt at mastery. Your partner may not be able to accomplish a task as efficiently as you do. Your role is not to involuntarily conform them to your way but rather to give them the space to discover what works best for them.

You could even take it a step further and ask how you can support their method. There are few things more humbling than becoming a servant to a vision that is not your own. This is only effective if you're able to truly serve their vision without feeling like you're being held against your will or cringing at the way they'd like things done.

I'm not suggesting that you would ever do this, but there are some people who serve other people's visions with an attitude so thick and heavy that it would be better for everyone if they didn't do it at all. When you connect with someone and have the heart to serve their vision, you posture yourself to become a student to different methods of accomplishing tasks.

I've had to grapple with this pride in every area of my life, from parenting to team building. There's a certain way I believe the household should be run. It checks all the boxes that are important to me, and I often run myself ragged trying to get it done. When I enlist my husband to help, I try to bite my tongue while he navigates the morning routine his way.

When I finally stopped measuring his effort to my expectation, I was able to learn the ways he does things differently than I do. Okay, I'll be honest. Some things aren't different—they're actually better, but let's keep that between us because I'm not ready to boost him up that much. I'm kidding . . . sorta.

I noticed almost immediately that though he's not massaging and easing the girls out of the bed in the morning to start the day, they're much more efficient when he's doing school runs. They negotiate with me but are much more responsive with him. My organizations are full of different project managing styles, and while I don't always agree with their methods, I have to acknowledge that they've been able to introduce systems and structures that have helped streamline productivity.

Pride is arrested when you relinquish the goal of being larger than what has happened in your life and instead embrace that because our lives are interconnected, everything we do is larger than just one life. It should make space for the reality that all lives are intersected, and myopic thinking is the easiest way to sever ties with others and become an island.

THE POWER OF THE COLLECTIVE

By the time you're reading this I will have hosted one of the largest events of the women's empowerment movement I founded, Woman Evolve. But right now I'm in the throes of planning, and it has been kicking my tail. Sometimes I am so consumed with how taxing it has been on me that I've thought, *I can't wait until this is over.* Two things immediately happen that instantly change my exasperation into exaltation—gratitude and hope.

The first thing is that I'm not pulling this off on my own. When we are consumed with our workload it can make it challenging to recognize that we're not pushing the ball forward alone. There is *nothing* that happens in our lives that is not affected by someone else's choice and/or decisions. Whether we like to admit it or not, we are experiencing our societies, projects, and responsibilities as a collective.

This truth means there is a possibility that there is someone whose plate is just as full as mine and yet they're finding a way forward too. It also means that nine times out of ten my plate is also lighter because of a load someone else is carrying. Ignoring the collective makes it more difficult for us to honor and value the people in our world who are giving us momentum.

There are people who are directly connected to the orchestration of your reality. They are government leaders, tech innovators, and business tycoons. I tell you right now that there is no praise like an Amazon same-day delivery praise. This is not just a convenience; it's an opportunity to acknowledge how much better our lives are because we're functioning as a collective.

It's easy to see how negative behaviors have an adverse effect on our reality. But how often do we intentionally celebrate how the combined ingenuity of a few can create exponential impact on many? That's what I know is going to happen at our annual event, even if that means we're dozing in the corner while everyone else is getting blessed.

The second thing that has been keeping me going is what I know will happen in the room when the thousands of women we're hosting come together. I am presently most excited about the worship that will fill the stadium. A place most commonly used to announce innings and home runs will become a resting place for healing, connection, restoration, and

God's glory. How is it possible that it can be flowing with alcohol and hot dog wrappers one weekend and become a house of worship the next? The power of the collective shifts even the most challenging atmosphere.

It is impossible to do anything on Earth without partnership. Even God partnered with a woman to bring salvation. Navigating the complexities of life will require strategic alliances and partnerships. When those partnerships share the same goal, nothing can stand in their way. Imagine how far you could go if you were wisely seeking the right partner to help catapult your vision.

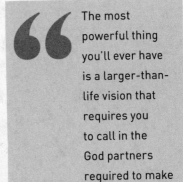

The most powerful thing you'll ever have is a larger-than-life vision that requires you to call in the God partners required to make it happen.

If I were you, I'd start defining the type of person your vision requires now so that you don't miss them when they come. If it's a romantic partner, what are their values? If it's a business partner, what skill set will they bring to the table that expands your vision? If you can't name it, you can't claim it. But if you can claim it, you can multiply impact. The most powerful thing you'll ever have is a larger-than-life vision that requires you to call in the God partners required to make it happen.

Flip the Switch

———————— **MARINATE** ————————

Do you have the power to make room for another person's method,
personality, and skills in the area where you're still developing?

———————— **ACTIVATE** ————————

Take note of the different ways people accomplish the same goal as
you and compliment their methods.

———————— **PRAY** ————————

*God, open my eyes to the ways You use different people to meet the same
objective. Help me to honor them the way You do.*

CHAPTER 12

JOINING FORCES

I HAVE NOTICED OVER THE COURSE OF THE LAST DECADE OR SO THAT businesses are more frequently joining together to maximize impact and increase brand awareness. When two brands offer different products or services that serve the same consumer, joining together creates efficiency and excitement that cannot be ignored. A great example of this happening is when GoPro joined forces with Red Bull.

I'm going to be honest and let you know that I already know that I am not their target demographic. My idea of adventure is spontaneously asking the older kids to watch the younger kids while I go eat a meal in the car. Their demographic is more on the jumping-out-of-an-airplane side of things.

Still, I marveled at how well the two brands understood their audience enough to join forces and create a campaign that encapsulated their shared value of reimagining the limits of human potential. Those shared values became the springboard that allowed them to create a project that expanded their imprint.

We've talked a bit about creating your own core values, but now we get to utilize those core values to help you better engage and support the people in your world. Part of the reason we struggle with truly maximizing the beauty of partnership and relationships is that we spend too much time filling a void instead of qualifying the material that we're using.

It will be no surprise to you that as an internet interior designer, I love HGTV. I am always captivated by how they take empty spaces and make them much more practical and aesthetically beautiful. What's even more meaningful is seeing the homeowner come back into their newly renovated home with gratitude because someone was able to transfer what was important to them into their personal space.

The interior designer understands that success was not about just filling the space with trinkets and things, but rather filling the space based on the values of the individual they were serving in the moment. The process can be tedious and may require patience, but being unrelenting in making sure the person's desires show up in the home is worth the wait.

I use this as an example of how we are in relationships with others, because if we make decisions based on filling a void of friendship, companionship, or productivity, we will be frustrated when the person does not share our values and begins to overdeliver in areas that don't matter while underdelivering in the spaces we care about the most.

If you're going to join forces with someone, you have to trust that you and the person have the same shared values. You must believe that the partnership will allow for you to become better and not thwart your growth and development. While there are countless examples of strategic partnerships in Scripture, I am not sure there is one that speaks to the power of joining forces like Jesus and His disciples.

First of all, can we take a moment and acknowledge that Jesus "The Force" Christ still joined forces with the disciples in order to get things done? Baby, if that doesn't humble you, I don't know what will. Jesus in all of His magnificence and glory did not start His ministry without first taking the time to make sure that He would not have to go at it alone.

Sure, there were moments when no one could fulfill the task but Him, like when He was on the cross. However, the moments we see Jesus alone in ministry are rare compared to the moments when He had at least His trusted three disciples with Him. Jesus recognized that the backgrounds of His disciples would be instrumental in realizing the larger-than-life mission that was ahead of Him.

He did not choose the first twelve people who signed up. He didn't even just put them to work immediately. Jesus journeyed with the disciples first. I believe that part of His inviting the disciples to follow Him was due to His wanting to get to know them before granting them access and bestowing them with power.

Before even giving them a task, Jesus granted them the power of access. Imagine how much differently we would handle our hearts if we realized it's not just about what someone does with their access that is powerful, but rather that the access itself is power. When you give someone access, you are beginning the process of joining forces with them. Having the patience to experience what they do with their access to you before assigning them to a sacred space in your world can save you frustration in the long run.

You don't have to jump the gun on filling the void just because you think you may have prospective material in an opportunity or candidate. Taking the time to understand a person's values and how they align with your own can ensure that when you join forces you become stronger. There's nothing that God is going to do on earth that will not require you to join forces, because everything that will be accomplished is too large for one life.

Becoming vulnerable to people is not my favorite hobby, but I'd be lying if I said I haven't reaped the rewards of falling back so someone else can come forth. In the process of doing that I've been able to increase and expand the vision God's given me for my life, family, gifts, talents, and influence in a way that would not have been possible without joining forces.

Even my books are an example of what happens when a message is amplified through the support of others. I wonder what could be amplified in your life by you joining forces. Could your peace be amplified by joining forces with someone else who shares your values? What about your bottom line in your business?

There's a story in the Bible about two women named Mary and Elizabeth. Both of them experienced miraculous pregnancies. When Mary learned she was going to conceive even though she'd never been with a man, the angel of the Lord told her that Elizabeth, her much older cousin, was miraculously pregnant as well. Once Mary moved from a place of fear to faith, she accepted the responsibility of partnering with God to change the world through her pregnancy.

> There are some battles that we must face alone, but then there are other battles where we must resist isolation if we're going to have victory.

What happened next has always moved me because it speaks to the power of women coming together. Instead of isolating herself and waiting for the miracle to become a reality, she went to see her cousin Elizabeth. I believe the angel of the Lord made it a point to make sure that Mary knew there was someone else who understood the responsibility of being a force with a miracle in the making.

There are some battles that we must face alone, but then there are other battles where we must resist isolation if we're going to have victory. Pay attention to the moments when God places someone in your world who is walking a similar path as you. There is power in joining forces with someone who is determined to not miss anything God has for them.

You may be looking for friends who share similar interests and that's okay, but when it comes to your destiny and the battleground where your fear and faith are facing off, you need someone who understands the power of God to make something happen that others deemed impossible. When we take advantage of the wisdom that is available to us from those God has placed in our lives, it is not a sign of weakness—it is a show of unstoppable force.

CONFLUENCE OVER INFLUENCE

When I first began blogging I'd receive countless comments from people proclaiming that I was their big sister. I've noticed over the last couple of years that unbeknownst to me I must have graduated, because when younger people reach out to me now they call me Auntie. I like to think that the twenty-year-olds calling me Auntie have done so because I'm the cool, young aunt who won't get upset when they tell them their secrets. However, the first five words of the next sentence and the paragraph that follows may betray my cool, young aunt status.

When I was growing up we only had models, movie stars, and music icons. Nowadays, when I log on to my social media and a person has a significant following, it's unclear how they became prominent. The emerging lane of individuals who have built an audience by sharing their vlogs, DIY hacks, recipes, gifts, talents, and unique perspectives on art and culture are called *influencers*.

Influencers have gone on to move into various segments of traditional arts and entertainment and have become forces to be reckoned with in securing brand and sponsorship deals once exclusively reserved for notable figures in film and entertainment outlets. There's no doubt in my mind that many of the opportunities I've been afforded would not have been possible without the pioneering work of influencers who became beloved to the communities they serve.

Still, as powerful as influencers have become, this is as misleading as the supernova stars of my youth. I call it misleading because though we only saw the people on the big screen or stages, they did not get there on their own. Behind every great person who achieved fame was a studio, label, or company that offered their strengths to the talent's gifting.

The influencer takes a similar journey. There comes a point when they recognize that the only way for them to leverage their platform to create more meaningful impact is through strategic alliances and partnerships. Whether their goal is to bring awareness to a philanthropic endeavor or to launch a business in order to fill those voids, an influencer must consider connecting with an organization that can accelerate their mission.

In nature, there is a similar phenomenon that involves two flows coming together to create a more powerful force. It's called a confluence. Geography teaches us that a confluence is when two rivers join together in order to form a single channel. When this single channel forms, the two rivers no longer exist as singular flows but rather two streams that have come together to create an even more powerful current.[9]

The most famous example of this occurrence is the Amazon River. The two rivers that join together to make the Amazon River are the Solimões and the Negro.[10] I can't help but marvel at the irony that the Amazon River is more known than either of the two rivers that join together to form it in the first place. You already know as a preacher I can't pass up the lesson in this moment. It's possible that what's on the other side of partnership is so undeniably powerful that every version of who you were before the confluence is small in comparison.

These two rivers join together in the Brazilian city of Manaus and form the famous Amazon River that we all know today. Imagine, if you can, what would have happened had the two rivers never converged. There's nothing that necessarily indicates that the rivers would have dried up or become depleted. There is no evidence that suggests that the two rivers would've gotten stronger individually and gone on to rival the impact of the Amazon River.

If we personify these rivers, we can imagine that they would have had to confront and overcome the many societal and personal barriers that deter us from converging with other forces. Fear of losing individualism and distinction or the concern that they weren't as qualified as the other river may have been realities. In geography, confluence is involuntary, but not so much in our spiritual, emotional, and relational journeys.

Too often we run the risk of staying in the flow of being individual rivers. We're so content with staying in our own flow that we miss out on the unique gift that occurs when two forces come together. Connecting with another person who is moving with the same sense of purpose, destiny, peace, and power as you is how humans experience confluences. Even deeper, merging our lives with God's will is a more transformational "river" than any confluence on Earth. Quiet as it's kept, that can be just as scary as intertwining our being with another person.

Joining forces with another person requires that we confront the fear of being lost in their story. Even once a person has shown themselves aligned with our values and intentions and proven that they can add strength to us in areas where our best could become better, the joining relies on an unnatural trust. I wonder what would happen if we actively engaged with the people in our world by analyzing whether the proposed engagement is forming a confluence or zapping us of power.

Let me be clear: qualifying our inner circle with a measuring stick of confluence is not about taking advantage of people. It's about understanding and valuing what you bring to the table. I'll tell you that it's not as challenging to evaluate the ways a person can make you better as it is to determine the ways you can add value to them. That's why it's critical to have a healthy knowledge of your flaws and strengths.

You have the ability to add value no matter what you've gone through, and you deserve to have a standard for what brings you health, safety, and security in your relationships. If you are unable to embrace the necessity of being strategic about whom you give access, you will find yourself constantly recycling similar toxic or draining connections.

Don't allow your openness to random people and connections to become a threat that leaves you stagnant. You're qualified to observe and analyze another person's flow because of how hard you fought to find your own flow and how protective you are about growing from there.

THE ULTIMATE CONFLUENCE

I am trying to help you understand the dynamics of how your connections create momentum for a powerful existence. Having criteria for the behaviors, conversations, and ethics you desire from the people you allow in your circle reduces the margin of confusion, disagreement, betrayal, and error. If you have to force the connection, the connection is not helping you become a force.

Almost all of the Old Testament follows the path of two rivers desperately attempting

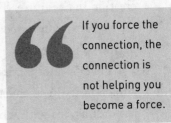

> If you force the connection, the connection is not helping you become a force.

to create a confluence to change the earth. The river of humanity and divinity engaged in a tangled waltz of a dance that often yielded disappointment. No matter how much God desired to truly dwell with His people, His people could not trust that their partnership with God was more than enough without additions. The beauty of the New Testament is the lengths that God was willing to go for His creation to experience the ultimate confluence.

If we can truly wrap our minds around merging with God, we will understand the foundational framework for every relationship we possess. You should make it a part of your routine to find time to live in the reality that the all-powerful, all-knowing, and ever-present God desires to dwell with you. He is there regardless of your weaknesses, ignorance, or disengagement.

I won't lie. The acceptance of that truth is humbling, convicting, and overwhelming. It renders you vulnerable, because God would rather have a trickle from you than nothing at all. God longs to unleash a divine stream of love and wisdom that radically changes your identity. If you're like me, it makes you feel overwhelmingly loved and undeserving.

At my core, I don't have any qualms with this, because if God's love doesn't overwhelm you and make you fall to your knees in gratitude, then His love would be like all the others. You could argue with God about choosing another stream other than you. Chile, God already knows that sometimes you're a shallow puddle on a busy city street compared to His rushing stream of grace and mercy.

Your job is not to get God to change His mind about you. Your job is to search God's mind for His truth about you. How do you search the mind of God? Of course, you can study how God engages with His creation in Scripture. That has proven to be incredibly instrumental for me and truly underscores what we've been learning about observing a person's character.

There is another, more intimate option, however, that relies on your vulnerability. You must first begin by assessing the areas where your mind disagrees with what you've heard about or experienced from God.

Where is the disconnect between who you understand God is and who you are? When you begin to confront the area where there is separation between you and God, you directly attack the space that doubt, fear, and dark forces exploit.

For example, many people struggle to believe that God is good all of the time because not everything in their life has felt good. This struggle is intensified the more they engage in choices they define as not being good. The problem is that when it becomes difficult to believe God is good, it also becomes nearly impossible to fully, truly trust God's plan for your life.

If that disconnect point becomes the starting point for a journey of seeking and finding, it opens your heart to receive the wisdom of God's goodness and how it has been showing up in your life even when you didn't see it. Just because I feel we may have stumbled into something, if it is your testimony that you're unsure of God's goodness, I'd like to leave you with a thought to consider.

Saying "God is good" is not the same as saying "life is good." God being good is the realization that good has a source and the source is God. Just like the ocean is blue and the sky is black at night, God is good. The substance of what God is made of is so good that even when good faces off against evil, it still turns out good. Your invitation to God to meet you, no matter where you are, is inviting good to take over your life.

> Your invitation to God to meet you, no matter where you are, is inviting good to take over your life.

When good takes over, doubt has to leave. When good takes over, bad loses its sting. When good takes over, the battles are no longer yours. When good takes over, obedience is not a chore but a privilege because you trust where you're headed. When good takes over, it empowers you even when life isn't going as planned because you recognize that your life is not your own, but rather a confluence of God's goodness and your weakness working together so that heaven can touch Earth.

Flip the Switch

MARINATE

Consider ways that current connections have organically become a confluence that has indelibly shaped you for the better into who you are today.

ACTIVATE

Research individuals within your personal community or online who are excelling in the area where you are developing. Connect with them directly or through their work. Choose one piece of advice or wisdom they provide and begin to apply it to your life.

PRAY

God, open my heart to receive the divine connections that will make me better. Help me to see the honor and privilege in the role I get to serve in helping others.

CHAPTER 13

OPEN YOUR MIND

SINCE I AM ALREADY WELL DOWN THE PATH OF NO LONGER BEING THE cool big sister and have ventured into Auntie land, I might as well go ahead and dive deeper into how much the world has changed from when I was growing up. As a millennial I entered the world in the middle of a cataclysmic shift. The introduction to the internet was still very fresh and exciting. AOL was the most popular domain for anyone with an email address, and computers had a backside so wide and large that they needed Spanx.

If I were telling you about the moments in my life when my parents exemplified the exact opposite of what it means to be a gentle parent, I would divulge what happened in the wee hours of the morning when I was caught sneaking into their office. Let's just say that the AOL chatrooms and my curiosity could have led me into some serious trouble.

While my parents did not go out of their way to sit down and talk to me gently about my proclivity to rebellion and mischief, they did help me to remember that the computer wasn't the only thing with a backside. They became more diligent about making sure their office door was locked so they could sleep without fear of my antics, and that was enough to curb my curiosity.

They would have needed a few more tricks up their sleeves if they were raising me today. Now, keeping your children off the internet requires much more than locking a door. The web is so readily available and accessible that my seven-year-old wants to know whether our destination has Wi-Fi before she hops in the car to run errands with me. She could probably not fathom that the only entertainment we had in the car as kids was trying to count how many cars we could spot that were the same color.

My husband tells a story of attending a technology conference right before the dot-com boom. He shares that a presenter was expressing to the crowd that there would come a time when people's lives would not be attached to a desktop computer or even a laptop, but instead a handheld device that could fit in their pocket. Touré shares that the crowd was in utter disbelief at the notion.

I don't want to spoil the ending for you, but I will say that it's highly probable that the archaic ancestors of the stunned audience are probably the people who laughed at Noah as he built the ark. Isn't it crazy how an idea can seem absolutely ludicrous one moment and then become absolutely essential over time?

I want to talk to you about what happens when you're the only one who can discern that power is moving from one way of being to another. We've talked about power moving between our internal thoughts and emotions. We've even discussed the power struggle between humanity and darkness, but as you begin to truly embrace your identity as a force on earth, I want to prepare you for what it feels like to be on the edge of innovation.

Few people truly discuss the loneliness, vulnerability, and second-guessing that come with being the first to see that power is shifting from one idea to another. I'll be honest with you, when this occurs, it's difficult to not feel like you may need to check yourself into a secluded retreat.

When you draw closer to God it doesn't just initiate a journey of bearing God's image on Earth; it also grants you access to God's plans for the earth. I wish I could explain this better. It's kind of like when you're an adult and a child asks you a question that you aren't capable of answering completely.

It's not that you don't know the answer; it's that you aren't sure the child could handle the answer because they have not developed enough to comprehend the complexity of it. When you begin to grow in God, God can share more about the complexities and nuances of His plan.

There's a scripture that sums this up perfectly. Proverbs 25:2 says, "It is the glory of God to conceal a matter, but the glory of kings is to search out a matter." This verse gives us insight into how God functions. Of course, when we think through the lens of our personal experiences, it's not a complete shock that God conceals things. Lord knows there have been plenty of moments when I've been completely in the dark about God's plans.

When I set aside the time, though, to truly seek the Holy Spirit in those dark seasons, I often find wisdom about why God allowed them, or didn't intervene, when I was at my lowest. Sometimes what you're calling darkness, God is calling development. It's the second part of this scripture that intrigues me because it puts the onus on an individual to not accept that darkness is the end.

> " Sometimes what you're calling darkness, God is calling development.

When you refuse to believe that you serve a God who would leave you in the dark, you search scriptures, sermons, worship songs, and meditations until you begin to see light flickering again. The pursuit of God's perspective is not just about reconciling your past and making peace with your present. God's perspective also carries with it innovation for how your gifts and talents align with what God wants to see happen in the earth.

YOU'RE ON TO SOMETHING

In communities of faith it's not uncommon to hear someone share that God "spoke" to them. As a child (okay, I'll be honest, even as an adult) the concept leaves a lot of room for questions. Hearing from God is not the same as the phone ringing or a ping going off to let you know a message has come through. Fine-tuning your heart and spirit to understand when God is speaking takes real intentionality and time.

Do you remember those awkward moments when you'd accompany your parents to an event with their friends? Random men and women would approach you and marvel at how much you've grown since they saw you twenty or thirty years ago. They make sure to let you know that they remember when you were "knee high to a grasshopper."

Before it becomes annoying, the first couple of times it occurs is actually interesting. A parent usually steps in to help jog your memory, and suddenly your interest blossoms. There's something powerful about someone knowing you long before you actually knew you. The sincerity in their words when they connect the characteristics they witnessed in your youth to the superpowers in your adulthood can be affirming and validating in ways you didn't even realize you needed.

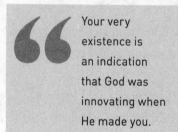

Your very existence is an indication that God was innovating when He made you.

These encounters are similar to what happens when we begin to truly experience a relationship with God. I'm going to give you a powerful thought to pray and meditate on as you begin to see how *your very existence is an indication that God was innovating when He made you.* Whew! That last sentence blessed my life because I know that it's true.

If you need evidence to ground my claim, you don't have to look any further than the reality of your DNA. The imprint of you that began formulating in your mother's womb was God curating an identity for you that would literally be unlike anything the world has ever seen. You, yes you, with all of your doubt, worry, and fear, were cutting-edge long before you took your first breath.

Embrace the truth that your existence is innovation. Your ideas that feel weird, quirky, and maybe a little strange are actually evidence that you're allowing your mind the freedom to live outside of constructs that exist to create conformity.

I am not suggesting that every single idea you possess is something that the world needs, because we all know that sometimes we have more ideas than we even have the energy, resources, or time to execute. I am proposing, though, that you become more comfortable with letting your mind run wild without fear of rejection or the awareness of its oddity.

When you shut your mind down before it can even get started you shackle it to an existence that can be neither broad nor expansive. Research has shown that allowing ourselves time to be bored is the best way to ignite our minds and imagination.[11] We are overstimulated from the moment we wake up to the second we lie back down.

Most of our stimulation is the byproduct of us living within the confines of someone else's imagination. You will never discover the power of your own ideas if you're constantly trapped living in someone else's. Even if it's just for ten minutes a day, you should take the time to free your mind. Now, some of you are going to need guardrails for this exercise because when you start letting your mind run wild it steers you towards doubt and creates more space for your anxiety.

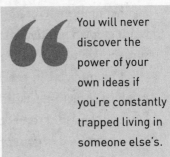

> You will never discover the power of your own ideas if you're constantly trapped living in someone else's.

Instead, I want you to free your mind in the direction of divine creativity. You have spent enough time playing devil's advocate when it comes to ideas about your health, finances, relationships, and destiny. Start challenging yourself to redirect your creativity in the direction of infinite possibilities.

I am reminded of when the disciples presented Jesus with a problem: a soon-to-be-hungry multitude of five thousand. They didn't even count how many women and children were there, and I'm not sure why because there's nothing more chaotic than a hungry woman and child. The disciples wanted Jesus to send them away, but Jesus refused and told the disciples to feed them instead.

The fellas drew a blank. They had no idea how they were supposed to respond to what seemed to be an impossible request, but because Jesus said they could do it, they had to take a minute and stretch their minds towards the possibilities they may have never considered.

Jesus did not just want them to solve a problem with what had already been done. He wanted them to solve a problem with what had never been done before. To be a true disciple of Jesus you must consider that the solution to the problems you do see may exist in a realm you do not see. It's not enough to see a problem if you don't trust that God has a solution worthy of searching His heart for.

Let's think of the craziest problem in your world right now. Did you just roll your eyes thinking about it? Because if you didn't, go find me another problem. Got it? Good! Now grab a pen and some paper and start writing down positive solutions to the problem. When you do this, make sure the solution connects in some way to your present circumstance.

The miracles in the Bible that we read about over and over never involved something falling out of the sky from nowhere. They always involved the use of something that was already in reach. It's true you don't know how God is going to solve the problems you see, but what if you started seeing everything in your life as a bridge to a miracle?

How differently would you treat it? What peace would be immediately available to you? Take the time to start wildly imagining the possibilities, and please note that the solution may be just as crazy as the problem. If you don't believe me, remember the disciples took a little boy's lunch and still had leftovers.

INNOVATION MINDSET

Do you think the person who invented the idea of flying cars did so while they were navigating their commute with ease? I'll be honest, I don't know who first had the idea of flying cars, but I'm willing to bet that I know how they came up with it. I imagine they were sitting in bumper-to-bumper traffic when they thought, *I wish this car had wings.*

Before you start trying to convince me you're owed money because you've had that thought, I want to remind you that it's not enough to have the idea if you're not going to take the time to let your mind and hands wander into the possibilities of how to make it happen. I'm not trying to pull anyone's resume, but I'm sure the people behind the invention of the flying vehicle didn't just have the idea but also the skills to turn it into a reality.

For most of us the idea was nothing more than a random thought that scrolled through our mind, but for someone else it launched a deep dive into a world of mechanics and engineering that produced a design so comprehensive that the FDA approved it for flight time.

I am trying to help you unlock the confidence that allows you to see that complicated problems often have equally complex solutions. Don't let that discredit the power of your curiosity to pave the way for innovation.

The example I've referenced may seem far-fetched for a person who is not a math whiz, but the truth is that innovation is not just trailblazing in the field of engineering and technology. You have an opportunity to innovate in your day-to-day life as it relates to your interpersonal relationships, financial and time management, and wellness goals.

I've recently discovered another area of personal development. I'm often lauded by my friends and family for my patience. I usually think nothing of it, but I've come to pay attention to when I feel particularly impatient, and it doesn't happen often. When it does happen there's usually one thing that's the culprit: complaining.

I. Am. Not. A. Fan. I have one husband, six children, two parents, and four siblings, and I lead a team of a few dozen people, so suffice it to say I have not found a way to rid my environment of complaining. Instead, I've learned to get to the root of why it irritates me and pray that God grants me more patience.

If I get into the full nuances of why it bothers me, we'll need a part 2 of this book, but one of the reasons is that I expect people to not just be vocal about what's wrong, but to offer ideas on how to make it right. Even if the answer isn't workable or feasible, if you stop at complaining, you've just dumped a problem onto my already full plate.

God is working on my patience by having me challenge the person who's presented a problem to also be innovative in finding a solution. It works like a charm when I'm able to do it without an attitude. When my seven-year-old comes to me in a panic because her older siblings won't spend time with her, I don't minimize her feelings or distract her with something else to do. I guide her in giving expression to what she feels so that she has the capacity for innovation.

Once her emotions have settled, I ask her, "What can you do with the time you wanted to spend with them?" Once we work through her initial meltdown, she begins to consider Barbie and tea party alternatives. My goal is to show her that as long as she has her mind she's never without possibilities.

It's not until she's forced into a position to weigh outcomes besides frustration and rejection that she's able to see a possibility that doesn't end in defeat. How many times have you settled into rejection when there's an opportunity for you to stretch your mind into possibilities? What power and talents are lying dormant in you because you've allowed a complaint to become a conclusion?

Innovation is not a one-time thing reserved for the next big invention. Innovation is a muscle that we have the opportunity to exercise each day if we're willing to think outside of defeat. Your mind is the most powerful weapon you possess. When nurtured properly it can empower you to unlock limitless potential. With all its power it's still relatively fragile, and with one experience or thought you can find yourself distrusting of yourself and stagnant.

When you transition to living with an innovation mindset, the impossible no longer feels too out of reach. The problems you see are opportunities to stretch your mind towards establishing new pathways for efficiency and success. Innovation that requires you to speak poorly of what came before you is a lethal combination of bitterness and creativity that will never truly satisfy your soul.

You'll know that your innovation has the potential to be fruitful when it is rooted in gratitude for the present and passion to transform the future problems before they even arise with solutions. When you innovate from a place of peace, your power maintains a healthy flow. You'll notice that as you begin to expand your mind with innovative thinking, your thoughts won't be the only things that change.

Your conversations will too. When that happens, your social circle may change too. I probably should have warned you before I started sharing about changing your mind, but better late than never to inform you that a transitioned mind must often say goodbye.

Flip the Switch

What is something you use or do every day that has become your norm but at one time would have been considered innovative?

Innovate your way through frustration. The next time you feel stuck, let your mind run wild with possibilities of how you could change your reality.

God, help me to recognize that with You I am never stuck. Awaken me so I can see where I can break through instead of break down.

CHAPTER 14

CHANGING CONNECTIONS

OUR WORLD IS DESIGNED TO REDUCE US TO FIT IN PARTICULAR CAT-
egories. When people are trying to get to know you, they aren't just
interested in diving deep into who you are. Most people are trying to
determine what type of person you are. Once they've identified the type
of person you are—shy, fashionable, athletic, smart, fun loving, clumsy,
funny, forgetful, moody—they build walls around you and expect you to
stay in the category that they understand.

One of the greatest gifts I've given myself is the freedom to be the
complex creature God created. I'm funny and serious. I am brave and
afraid. I am powerful and insecure. I am strong and vulnerable. I am who
I was, who I am, and who I am becoming all at the same time. If you
were to be honest, you'd admit to being a polarized figure too.

It is crucial for you to fully comprehend
the reality of your inheritance of power
through your relationship with Jesus. When
you refuse to live within the box that people
have relegated you to, you cultivate relationships to become as fluid as the power you
flow in. If a person is going to be connected
with you, they're going to have to be able to
move and flow as you do. Any relationship

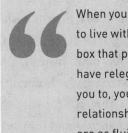

When you refuse
to live within the
box that people
have relegated
you to, you force
relationships that
are as fluid as the
power you flow in.

that requires you to be stagnant will frustrate you because the connection feels like restriction at a time when pursuing freedom has become your passion.

Imagine there are two types of people in your life: people who flow with your power and people who can only handle one version of you. Believe it or not, they are both equally necessary for your spiritual health and well-being.

Let's use Jesus as an example. The disciples consistently stayed with Jesus throughout His ministry. Jesus was full of power and led by power while He fulfilled His time on the earth. The disciples weren't just observers of what was happening in His life. They also weren't sycophants who were chasing the clout of His fame.

The disciples were connected to Jesus because being in His flow awakened them to the possibilities of how their connection with God was a river waiting to be released into the earth. Before Jesus had the disciples, though, He had His mother, Mary. She flowed with Jesus up until His ministry began, and then we see a shift.

The woman who once flowed with Him was now floating sporadically throughout the scenes of His life. She was not as constant as the disciples, but occasionally we see her drifting by in pivotal moments. Mary gave Jesus the space He needed to innovate without requiring Him to stay accessible and reachable. She was only able to give Him this space as He walked in His power.

Fourteen years ago, a day or so after returning home from giving birth to my daughter, I went to the restroom, and when I stood up I fainted. My parents rushed me to the hospital where I fully expected to be taken to the pleasant labor and delivery staff I'd come to know over the last few days. Instead, I was taken to the emergency room and admitted into the regular hospital.

I thought for sure that the doctor who'd cared for me during my pregnancy would stop by to assess my status, but instead I was introduced to a new physician who would consult with my obstetrician as necessary while they determined the proper treatment plan. Once I got over the hormonally heightened sense of rejection and abandonment, it made sense as to why I wasn't on the floor with the new or expectant mothers.

I was no longer in a position to receive that level of attention and care because the labor and delivery phase of my journey was completed. My pregnancy doctor would be available if needed, but she may not have been qualified to handle the root cause of what caused me to lose consciousness. She'd flowed with me for almost ten months, but it was time for me and baby to move in a direction that would make our connection less frequent but no less meaningful.

Her nearby presence assured me that if I needed her she would be in reach, but if I insisted on her providing care I would lose valuable time getting to a place of wellness. This is what happens when we try to force someone to grow in the same direction and at the same rate as us. Forcing people to flow in currents they aren't called to creates opportunity for one or both of you to end up flailing when you could have been thriving.

It wasn't until Jesus stepped into the fullness of His ministry that disruption in His connection with Mary occurred. Disruption is not always dysfunction; sometimes it's a sign of development. It's impossible to stay the same and change at the same time. When Jesus went from possessing power to releasing power, it changed who He connected with in His social circle.

When you begin to put your power out there, you will be sounding an alarm to your friends, family, and community that the current of who you once were is shifting and you're flowing differently than you were before. When your innovation transitions from being more than a silly passing idea to a powerful plan in motion, you will be able to see clearly who can flow with you and who will be a member in your village who can't go with you but has enough wisdom to not hold you back.

Someone who can flow with you studies how you communicate, interact, disseminate, and retain your power so that they can support, expand, and restore you in the way you need it the most. The disciples were not just along for the ride. They were changing the tires, filling up the tank, cleaning the windows, and ready to get behind the wheel if necessary.

I won't lie to you and say it's easy to have peace when the people you wanted to flow with you make it evident that at most, all they can do is float by occasionally, but there is something to be said about trusting that the obedience God is requiring of you is worth the discomfort of flowing anyway.

What I love about trusting your relationship with God as the ultimate navigator for your life is that you don't just become confident and powerful, but you also become deeply compassionate. Abandoning your comfort zone and following God is hard work. It requires a lifelong commitment of living a vulnerable life. Seeing other people stuck in the crosshairs of fear and indecision makes you more sympathetic than judgmental.

I've had the opportunity to witness female survivors of domestic abuse serving women who are trying to determine whether they should leave. The survivor knows that there is liberty, safety, and joy on the other side of their decision but exercises compassion, because she also knows how hard it is to leave everything you've known no matter how toxic it is.

Tapping into transformation, regardless of where you're starting from, is an opportunity for you to be more delicate with people who are still finding their way. I am skeptical of people who profess to have encountered God's grace but fail at extending grace to others. When you truly recognize how arduous the process of being renewed and restored by God is, it should make you a safe space for others.

From a place of true humility you're able to recognize that you may be the one floating while someone you once felt close to flows on by. Even Jesus' life is a testament to this. Most of the disciples flowed with him for three years until He was on the cross.

Then there was Mary, the one whom He flowed by in a multitude, seated nearby while He hung from the cross; her presence serves as a reminder that just because a person could not flow with you in one thing doesn't mean they can't be there for you when you need them the most.

The reason why it's important to understand who has the capacity to flow with you versus float with you is because there will come a time when your idea must be shared with someone. You need valuable input with various perspectives to help you understand what part of your concept is viable and what's underdeveloped. We all have blind spots, and valuable input offers us a more thorough view of how to position what's in our hearts to have the maximum impact in the world.

There are countless times as a business owner and content creator that I've volunteered for the vulnerability that receiving input requires. My perspective has been challenged and expanded and, as a result, the impact has been significantly multiplied. I've learned to embrace input as an entrepreneur and I think that's because it's more commonly accepted, but the areas where I "should" have things figured out are the places where asking for input requires I quiet the nagging inadequacy that lives rent-free in my head. Can you relate?

The thought of asking someone for marital or parenting advice when it appears that it's coming easy for others has been difficult, but I've also learned that innovation without input is an idea waiting to crumble. If you think that innovation is reserved only for technology startups and business endeavors, you're depriving yourself from releasing the type of creativity that can make your life more manageable.

Let's think about that for a second. Whomever you're in relationship with—whether it's a friend, sibling, partner, child, parent, or colleague—is an individual so unique that their fingertips and DNA cannot be replicated. Why would we force a cookie-cutter way of connecting, loving, and supporting onto someone whom God has graced with that level of distinction?

When we choose to innovate in the ways of love, we're daring to ask the person we're committed to how to best show up in a way that matters the most to them. Wanting to be a good wife to Touré is a different standard than just wanting to be a good wife. And there's not a classroom more skilled at teaching innovative relational skills than parenting.

All it takes is more than one child before you begin to realize that what worked for one won't work for the other. I'm learning to make space for my individuality while protecting, serving, and developing my little humans into good people. Even though I'm a busy mom with a demanding travel schedule, I don't want my children's gifts and talents to be stifled by the availability of my schedule.

As a result, I end up saying no to more things than I say yes to, but there are still trips, projects, and tasks that I enjoy that take me away from them. Do I feel guilty for that? Sometimes. But I'm also honest enough to admit that there are moments when I've felt bitter because I denied my needs in order to be the kind of mom I'm "supposed" to be.

In a perfect world I'd attend every practice, rehearsal, recital, tournament, and presentation while not missing a meeting, recording podcasts, finishing manuscripts, preaching sermons, developing new ideas, and serving the teams that allow us to make indelible imprints on the world. I won't even get into getting eight hours of sleep, self-care, relationships, or eating for fuel and not enjoyment.

Well, Chile, the world isn't perfect and there's no way I can check all of the boxes. The first step in me allowing myself to introduce innovation into my rhythm, specifically as a mother, was communication. It sounds juvenile, but I discovered that I was often communicating from a place of burnout instead of being proactive about my capacity in advance.

Proactive communication begins with yourself before anyone else. You have to be willing to look at all of your tasks and responsibilities and determine what you desire to accomplish versus what you legitimately have the capacity to accomplish. I know you would do it all if you could, but you also know you can't do it all.

The sooner you can be honest with yourself about what's possible, the more quickly you can connect with those around you who may be able to offer you support. That may come in the form of friendship, family, or partnership. Make a daily practice of checking your inner fuel tank so you can determine exactly how far you can go before running out of patience, energy, and hope.

I know we're all responsible adults these days, but I also know a thing or two about running out of gas. The crazy part is that even though the car doesn't move, it doesn't mean it has no power. I want you to know that just because you have the power to start something doesn't mean you'll always have the fuel it takes to make sure it's complete.

Checking your inner fuel tank is a practice that sets the tone for your day, but I'll be honest, the sooner you can get ahead of it, the better. If you're able to look at your life a couple of days or even a week in advance, you're able to better pace yourself. Once you assess what's realistic for you to accomplish, you can readjust expectations of those affected—and that's when the innovation begins.

You get to go through each task and ask yourself, "Do I really have to do this, or am I doing it because it's what I'm supposed to do?" There's a moment in the Bible where Adam told God that he was hiding because he was naked, and God asked him, "Who told you that you were naked?" (Genesis 3:11). However you imagine God asking that question is how I want you to ask yourself, "Who told you you're supposed to do it this way?"

YOU'RE NOT A PUPPET

The questions you're asking are meant to restore your power as an individual and not a puppet. They are meant to serve you in assessing whether you are living up to your idea of what a business owner, partner, friend, or family member should be or if you are trying to force yourself to fit in the construct that your community created. Here's your chance to innovate!

More often than not I've found myself seeking to become powerful at being who others perceive me to be instead of living in the power of my truth and authenticity. Counterfeit power is built on the validation of

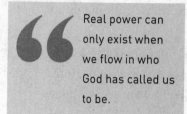

> Real power can only exist when we flow in who God has called us to be.

many. Real power can only exist when we flow in who God has called us to be.

When I realized that my desire to check all of the boxes of motherhood was rooted in wanting to play the role of a supportive mother instead of being the kind of mother that my children need *and* that I have the capacity to be, everything changed. Assuming this is a safe place, I'm going to go out on a limb and tell you something that may make you judge me a little: I have no desire to be at every little thing that my children have going on in their lives.

Now let me explain. It's not that I don't love them or care about what they do, but sometimes I need a break to do nothing and time to feel like a main character and not an extra. I learned that what I really want is for them to know that every little thing they do matters to me.

Communicating with them revealed to me that my physical presence is not the only way I can achieve that goal. Ironically, communication is also how I was able to achieve it and preserve the few nerves I had left on busy weeks. I interview them about their days like I'm Oprah in training. I ask every random thing when we get on the phone or they make their way home. Everything from *what did you eat for lunch?* to *did anything make you upset today?* I know most of their friends by name and make sure to follow up with them about the last week to see how things have changed.

When I'm traveling I help them understand that loving what you do and loving many people sometimes means you have to make tough choices. I use points of reference that they understand to express my absence.

"You know how you weren't able to come to church on Sunday to hear me preach because of your tournament? It's hard when we want to be in two places at once, but we know that no matter where we are, because we love each other we're always together. Next week I'll be out of town for your practice, but I want to hear all about how your serve is getting stronger."

I don't rob them from the right of being disappointed, nor do I expect them to always understand in the moment. Through communication we learn to honor our feelings and emotions and to support one another as family members and individuals. When all is said and done I want them to see that I was present significantly more than I was away and that the moments I was away were made up for in the way we prioritized innovative connection while apart.

They also know that they reserve the right to pull the "kid" card, and I'll drop anything even if they don't know exactly what it is they need. I would not have been able to detach myself from the expectations of motherhood and innovate a new way forward without taking the time to express and hear the values of my children.

Welcoming innovation into the dynamics of how you relate with others eliminates the need to give yourself or others ultimatums. Innovation is the gateway for compromise that feels mutually beneficial and not like one person got the short end of the stick. It helps to ensure that relationships maintain their equitability and closes the gap for burnout.

You have a lot going on in your world, and you're not always going to get it right. As a matter of fact, there will be moments when there's no room for innovation and all you can do is pray for the grace to survive the days ahead. In those moments I want to challenge you to get innovative with your prayers.

> "You have a lot going on in your world, and you're not always going to get it right.

It's still the same steps as before. You take the time to communicate with yourself and size up your responsibilities, but instead of turning to an individual to help, you ask God, with specificity, to send His Spirit to guide you in the places you fear depletion. I have learned that my prayer life has increased when my capacity does not measure up to the responsibilities at hand. Those are the moments when I get to pray and ask the Holy Spirit to fill my cup and order my steps.

Flip the Switch

MARINATE

Who are the people you were once flowing with but are now floating with, and vice versa?

ACTIVATE

Express your gratitude in person or through prayer for those who've managed to serve you in the different seasons of your life.

PRAY

God, help me to see where I may be holding someone hostage or interfering with their destiny. Allow me to become as generous with them as I need someone to be with me.

CHAPTER 15

FEAR LESS

THE FIRST TIME I HEARD THE POEM AT THE BEGINNING OF THIS BOOK I was watching a movie called *Coach Carter*. I'd never heard it before, and I was at a crossroads in my life where I was too young to truly understand the poem but also old enough to detect the truth in it. At its core the poet is challenging us to truly inspect the fear of being powerful.

It's interesting because on one hand if you're reading this book, even if you're not sure that it's possible for you, you're curious about what it would mean to have an identity marked by power. There's also likely the fear of the responsibility that comes with being powerful.

Being powerful is recognizing that your life has a predetermined impact that is meant to fill the world with love and goodness no matter how much pain and bitterness you have experienced. Your life matters to God's master strategy of reconciling His creation back to Him. I know not everyone reading this book is a Christian and yet, if you haven't guessed it by now, I definitely am.

The foundation of my faith is connected to my profound belief that following the life of Jesus is the only way to experience the fullness of God's plan for the earth and for you. When we model our life after Jesus, as children of God, we no longer represent just ourselves, but we represent God too.

We become a part of what Scripture calls a royal priesthood (1 Peter 2:9), and that makes us ambassadors of heaven who are on assignment on Earth. It's like joining a branch of the armed forces. No matter where you are from or who you were connected with before, what matters the most is the assignment connected to where you've been enlisted. If I can take it even further, I'll let you in on a secret. Low-key, you were enlisted before you even converted.

Jeremiah 1:5 lets us in on how God connects with His creation before they even take their first breath. Once we enter the world and are exposed to all of the things that make life beautiful and complicated, we have no recollection of those moments before our mother's womb.

Yet many of us come to suspect that there is more to life than the moment we're drowning in. The pursuit for salvation comes in many forms. Some find it in achievement. Others find it in drugs. Then there are the ones who look for it in alcohol. And let's not forget about the ones who try to find it in love.

We find different saviors along the way, but none of them leave us satisfied; we must discover true relationship with Jesus. I love an authentic church with trustworthy leadership, but that's not finding Jesus. A relationship with Jesus is a fully integrated faith that begins with a curiosity, a "trial" period, and then finally a real commitment.

I think it's important that we acknowledge these stages because when I was growing up I perceived that if I could not be on fire for God, there was not space for my flicker at all. So I want you to know what I learned later in life. For some, walking with Jesus is an overnight inferno that completely consumes their life.

Then there are those of us whose walk with Jesus begins with sentences like "If you're real, help me to really feel your presence." When having a faith that feels certain and sure is out of reach, a small mustard seed is enough for God to start working with. What's crazy is how I started uncertain and unsure, but now I know without a doubt that the power of God has shown up in my life in a way that cannot be explained away.

I'm not here to judge where you are on the journey, but I do want you to understand that the commitment stage of faith is not nearly as intimidating as choosing a spouse. With a partner you may wonder how they'll think or feel if your most shameful secret is revealed. Jesus already knows you're raggedy. Jesus isn't expecting perfection. Jesus could not care less about your dirty little secrets. For some crazy reason Jesus calls our scars beautiful and longs to see our slates wiped clean.

There is nothing more powerful than being radically loved by someone who is not surprised by your success and is compassionate when you're at your worst. When you do the work of allowing that kind of love to engulf you, it is so liberating that the words in the introductory poem resonate that much deeper.

Why would anyone be afraid of being powerful beyond measure? It's simple. To be powerful beyond measure is to break covenant with the ways you play it safe or small so that you don't experience failure. When you know you're powerful beyond measure you no longer plan your success and escape at the same time. You live as if failure is not an option. You force defeat to become your teacher, and your achievements are merely mile markers on the road to destiny because God's power is always moving you forward.

We're almost at the end of this journey together, and I want nothing more than to set you up to make the type of power moves that awaken you to an existence that is not held captive by the pursuit of perfectionism. Life is a messy job. You get to decide whether you allow that mess to help you or bury you.

BECOMING A HEAVYWEIGHT

In Matthew 25 Jesus shared a famous story, or parable, about the kingdom of heaven. I never like assuming that everyone knows what terms like the "kingdom of heaven" or "parable" mean, so I'll share with you the SJR definition.

The "kingdom of heaven" is a phrase Jesus used throughout Scripture to give context and insight to the listeners of His message into the way God relates to His creation. A parable is a metaphor built on concepts an audience understands for principles they're still trying to comprehend. The goal was to convert the hearers of the message to become citizens and then ambassadors for the kingdom of heaven on Earth.

Whenever there's a parable in the New Testament, there's usually an authority figure who is navigating the complexities of relationships or utilizing a person or group to complete a particular assignment. The one authority figure depicted in Matthew 25 was a master with three servants. The chapter shares with us that the three servants were each given "talents" from their master.

Before you start thinking that the master gave one impeccable rhythm and another the voice of an angel, that's not what talent means in this instance. The word "talent" used in the New King James Version was later translated as "bags of gold" in the New International Version of the Bible.

Even without the translation, reading the full account of the parable makes it pretty clear that the servants were given some type of currency, and they were expected to take what they were given and multiply it through investment. Two of the three servants were successful at multiplying their talents. The one who failed to increase the talent he was given was not unsuccessful because of a lack of effort.

The man was unsuccessful out of extreme caution. He did not want to risk losing what he'd been given and determined that at least returning what he had was better than taking the risk of losing it altogether. If we were actually talking about money, this may not have been the worst thing in the world, but remember, a parable is not a retelling of an actual event.

While I do believe there's something to be said about being a good steward of your finances and understanding how investments can make your money work for you, I believe the principle Jesus was sharing here is much deeper.

I perceive that Jesus was trying to teach us about the risk we must be willing to take to be fruitful in spreading the revelation of the kingdom of heaven. The principle that power is not reserved for a select few but is freely given to anyone who is willing to be led by the Spirit of God is not just a good idea—it's a revelation. The reality that your past does not define you and that Jesus doesn't just look past your flaws but literally looks right at them and still thinks you're to die for is a revelation.

This parable is showing us that the kingdom of heaven is like a master, God, who gave His servants, us, something that is too valuable to keep to ourselves. If you know that what you have comes from God, but you keep it within because you're afraid to fail, you are allowing what God has given you to bow down to fear. I hope this is serving as a news flash that fear has been sitting on the throne of your life for so long that you're forcing your anointing to bow down to it. The lesson that we glean from the man who hid his talent is that Jesus does not want us to hoard what we've been given.

God can't multiply what you won't sacrifice. The man with the talents was so afraid of failing that he missed out on the opportunity for multiplication. When the other servants proved that they could take what they'd been given and multiply it, they showed their master that they could endure the vulnerability that comes with risking failure.

> God can't multiply what you won't sacrifice.

The Greek word that was translated as *talents* in Matthew 25 actually means weight. In ancient Rome, money was not counted by dollars and cents but rather by weight. I found this fascinating because it helps me to understand the parable of talents even more.

The man who did not increase his talents ultimately did not add more weight to what the master had given him. The ones who were celebrated received praise because they managed to take the weight that was given to them and make that weight work for them.

Each of us enters this world with a weight to bear. Some of us may only have one burden while others may have so much load that it's bearing down on our shoulders. We all have moments when we become so distracted by what we're carrying that we miss out on the opportunity to make it work for us.

What if we spent less time trying to get rid of the weight we're carrying and more time trying to figure out why God chose us to carry it in the first place?

The parable of the talents reveals more than a principle about what's expected of us when we're a part of the kingdom of heaven. It also shows us that when we act like the man with one talent we're seeing ourselves less than how God sees us. The master was upset because he knew that the servant had what it took to let that weight turn him into a heavyweight.

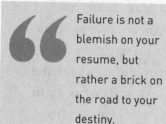

> Failure is not a blemish on your resume, but rather a brick on the road to your destiny.

You have to have a mindset that clings to the belief that failure is not a blemish on your resume, but rather a brick on the road to your destiny. You are going to fail. You're going to be brilliant at some things and terrible at others. You're going to start off terrible in something and become a master the more you practice.

I need you to begin to see past the devastation of failure and instead see it as a necessary tool that God uses to construct who He knows you can become. One of the many lessons from this parable is that what feels like a risk to you may be the only way you truly get to experience all God's placed inside of you.

STRADDLE THE LINE

I marvel at Jesus' ability to straddle the duality of His existence. He was completely human and completely divine. His ability to master living at this intersection should be the goal of how we spend our time on Earth. It's only possible when we are fully convinced of the divine necessity of our life on Earth. I will never get tired of reminding some and informing others that their life is not random. You were not created out of boredom or haphazardly.

It doesn't matter the context of your birth origin. Everything that God created has a purpose in His creation. Your father or mother may not have known what to do with you, but that doesn't change the fact that God has use for you. The tension of not being completely understood by the people in our environment is a source of trauma until we recognize that it's often why we triumph.

If you were completely understood, you would never seek to be exposed to environments that reflect externally what you feel internally. The hunt is ultimately the beginning of what allows us to truly tap into the image of God that we were designed to reflect. The greatest gift that you can give the people you love is the freedom to grow without being limited by your perceptions.

When we seek to experience people instead of controlling them, we become more like God in how we relate to them. Love is not just accepting someone for who they are; it's also accepting them for who they are becoming. I'm not sure it's possible to love someone with this type of dexterity unless you fully embrace that this kind of love is available in your relationship with God.

Jesus modeled this love in the way that He connected with the people He encountered in His ministry. He was able to be fully present with their suffering and fully hopeful for their future restoration. Jesus didn't just straddle the line of humanity and divinity, but He also straddled the line of the present and the future. I want us to learn to do the same.

Jesus knew that His journey was leading to the cross, but He did not shun all of the people, opportunities, and experiences that were on the way to the cross. Imagine Jesus ignoring the blind man yelling from the side of the street, the woman with the issue of blood, the men with leprosy, or any of the other miracles He performed.

Imagine if Jesus would've waited to find an empty cross and convinced someone to help Him fulfill the mission so He could just check the box as complete. It sounds ridiculous, because at the end of the day Jesus was not just meant to die for our sins. He served as an example of what a reconciled life with God looks like. Jesus entered each day with a focus on the future while remaining sensitive to the lessons hidden in each day.

While God is still revealing to you the plans and strategy for your future, you must trust and believe that the clues are hidden in your present. A healthy relationship with disappointment and failure is critical in assuming a posture of power while you're waiting on God's plan to unfold. Instead of seeing disappointment and failure as a delay or denial, you get to see it as divinely assigned to develop you or your surroundings for the future that God has not changed His mind about.

If your failures could change God's mind about you, He would never have sent His Son to save you. Each day—whether it's a day when your incompetence and inadequacy are on full display or a day when you feel so powerful that you're shocking yourself—is an opportunity to ask God what He's trying to show you about His character or yours.

When we straddle this fence in our relationships it allows us room to be frustrated but committed. In business we are able to be responsible for outcomes and for the culture our team functions in. My husband has a saying about the kingdom that constantly rings in my head. "We're not here to take sides. We're here to take over." It's difficult to give up when you embrace that two things can be true at one time.

I can be upset about what you did and in love with who you are. I can be intent on building what God's given me and compassionate towards those who don't understand it yet. The polarization that exists in most societies, and heavily in American culture, has caused many of us to believe that if we aren't choosing sides, we can't be effective.

I hold to the truth that we are to be in the world but not of it. Straddling the fence of being in it but not of it means there will be moments when we learn through mistakes and failure that we were leaning too far in one direction. Hindsight is a teacher that helps you to see clearly how to show up in power for your future.

Trust that the only win in life is living a life that reflects God's image on earth. Don't allow your win to be determined by how well you perform. Instead lean into a mindset of victory that is anchored in how many lessons you've learned. When you are anxious for nothing, you're able to be present in the moment and open for the impossible.

Flip the Switch

MARINATE

What failures have you experienced that left a mark on your confidence?

ACTIVATE

Share the lesson connected to that failure with someone who may not have known the aftermath you've overcome.

PRAY

God, I want to reject the spirit of fear that has kept me from soaring. Release Your Spirit to occupy the place where fear wants to control me.

CHAPTER 16

KNOW YOUR HARM

ANCIENT GREECE WAS ONE OF THE MOST DOMINANT INFLUENCERS OF the world. Its infusion could be found in the curation of art, food, textiles, farming, fishing, trading, and even medicine. Thousands of years have passed, and the essence of its impact is still foundational in many of these fields.

When I study the New Testament in its original language, I am taking a trip through a time machine. I study the historical context of when the manuscripts were written, and the Greek language in which it was presented.

The Grecian impact on our daily living is most evident in the field of medicine. Most of us are familiar with the Hippocratic oath that doctors vow even if we've never studied to be a doctor ourselves. The first iteration of this oath was written in Ionic Greek and dates back to somewhere between the fifth and third centuries BC.[12]

The oath is long and thorough in its intent to hold physicians to a standard of morality and ethics that seeks to serve each patient with wisdom, compassion, and innovation. There is a part in the oath that has become so popular that it's taken on different iterations over time:

> I will use those dietary regimens which will benefit my patients according to my greatest ability and judgment, and I will do no harm or injustice to them.

It is my wholehearted belief that most physicians who take this pledge do so with the intent of truly serving their patients to the best of their ability. I can imagine that as technology and science advances the medical field has been able to deepen their commitment to the philosophies expressed in the oath. I also realize that there's another truth that neither patient nor doctor can avoid.

Viruses and diseases are advancing and becoming more complicated almost at the same rate as technology and science—sometimes surpassing them. That's why doctors, though well-educated professionals, keep ever present the reality that they are yet practicing.

On one hand they are obviously knowledgeable with years of education, observation, and application under their belts, but they must also balance the power of their preparation with the reality of their ignorance.

Though they take a vow that they'll do no harm, they also recognize that the vow does not promise patients will always get the outcome they desire. It may not be the doctor's intent for the patient or family to experience harm in the process of their treatment, but intent and outcome are two separate experiences.

Some of you are practicing doctors. Thank you for the sacrifice you make to help us live our lives in optimum health. Others, like me, are not doctors, but we're still practicing at doing many (okay, most) things. Like a doctor, the potential for life-threatening results of our practicing exists.

Acknowledging that level of pressure can be crippling and deflating. I don't want to practice at being a wife, mother, daughter, sister, friend, or leader. I want to be a master at them all. Still, my life is laden with enough data that points to the reality that I am indeed practicing.

Many of us are learning to embrace the reality that we are not perfect and despite our best efforts we're likely to fall short, but I'd like to offer more expanse to this reality. You may not just fall short. You, regardless of your intent, may inflict harm on another individual.

That may feel disarming and unlikely given how desirous you are to see those in your life feel loved, appreciated, and valued. Normalizing our capacity to be both a victim and a villain is not something we often talk about. Back to the reality of polarization, we believe that we are entirely good or entirely bad, never contemplating that it's possible for us to be a cocktail of both.

A person who seeks to move with power is only able to do so when they discern when the power they've been granted transformed from a tool into a weapon and wounded an undeserving soul. There's nothing more powerful than being able to take accountability for where you've messed up so that you can grow. If you can't admit where you failed, you cannot reflect God's character on Earth.

Power without accountability will always turn to abuse. I believe that this is why Jesus was intentional about taking time away from His close circle to have solitude with God. It wasn't just about the necessary refreshing and restoration that comes from connecting with God. Prayer is an opportunity for God to fine-tune our spirit when we've become detached from how our actions are negatively affecting our ultimate goal or the people in our lives.

When a doctor's practice has damaging outcomes, they are held accountable and must undergo a malpractice investigation. When we have damaging outcomes, we're not always held accountable. Since most people have not been afforded the right to express disappointment without disconnection, they internalize or suppress the way our words and actions negatively affect them.

Of course, nothing we suppress or avoid actually goes away, and the inability to be held accountable negatively affects people we value and prohibits them from truly being able to grow in loving and serving the people they're in connection with. You can't always expect the people in your life to feel safe sharing the ways they experience your underdevelopment.

Harnessing the power to be seen by others with all of your beauty and flaws is one thing, but creating space for another imperfect person to share where you can be made whole is a skill that must be developed.

NO PERFECT TEACHERS

Who was your favorite teacher growing up? Did they teach a particular grade or subject? Chances are you did not have the same teacher from kindergarten to fifth grade. I'll take it a step further and wager that you didn't have the same teacher from kindergarten to middle school or high school.

I wish I could attribute that to prophetic insight, but truth is I've connected with enough teachers to know it's very rare that a teacher has the desire or ability to teach every single subject of every single grade.

It's not that they don't have the ability to increase their proficiency in order to cover more than one grade, but it's unlikely because they recognize that their teaching interest and style is more suitable for a certain subject and grade level.

I don't expect my daughter's history teacher to assist her with chemistry homework. He may be able to, but that's not a strength he's allowed us to observe. It would be foolish to believe that he's incapable of adding value at all just because that is not his strength.

It takes multiple teachers for a student to become a master. Likewise, it takes multiple teachers for a person to become a force. I want to prepare you for the reality that some of the teachers that God has assigned to your life are going to be imperfect. That may sound elementary, but it's important that you begin to accept that the teachers assigned to your life will also still be students in another area.

It's like an older sibling helping the younger with math. The older sibling is doing algebra and the younger is doing addition. They're both still learning, but one has learned enough to help the other. We often miss out on the opportunity to gain the advantage on our brokenness for immaturity because we reject teachers who are still in development too.

I've had to wrestle with not accepting feedback about my life from people who don't have their life together. It's true that some people were definitely giving me advice they weren't taking themselves, but I've had to ask myself to look beyond the source and test the validity of the advice against my relationship with God.

The first few years of my marriage I was notorious for doing this with my husband. You talking about somebody who would let him know to sweep around his own front porch. Chile, the man could not say a word! I could not keep my mind from thinking on all of the ways he could adjust and become better.

I kept it to myself and allowed it to take up space in our marriage until finally I realized that the divide could be filled by gently showing one another the ways we unintentionally harm others. Deflecting from the way that you harm someone and highlighting the way that they harm instead is a sign of immaturity that keeps you from truly being powerful.

A person who is powerful doesn't need for their teacher to be perfect in order to challenge them to grow. There was only one perfect teacher, and He's sitting at the right hand of the Father. The rest of us are down here doing the best we can to turn our wounds into lesson plans.

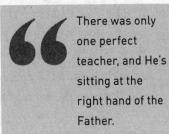

> There was only one perfect teacher, and He's sitting at the right hand of the Father.

Sometimes God uses the people around you to develop the gift of God in you. You owe it to who you desire to be in God to consider the way that other people experience you against the person you're aiming to become.

Remember when we talked about being innovative in the ways that we relate? After you visualize that innovation and dare to enact it in your life, the next step is quality assurance. That's when you make sure that you are living up to who you've set out to be to the people who you're serving, leading, or connecting with.

The only way to perform a quality assurance check is to open up the lines of communication with direct questions. Instead of asking, "Do you think I'm a good friend?" ask, "Do you feel that I'm loyal to you and supportive of your work?" Asking targeted questions opens the door for rebuking and/or recalibrating.

Introducing opportunities for active accountability creates a culture in your relationship for feedback about the ways that you can improve. When accountability is introduced it lays a foundation for trust and safety between individuals. When a person knows that you can handle the truth without punishing them for their experience, they feel safe enough to be authentic *and* corrected when needed.

Trust without accountability is an illusion. Exercising opportunities for accountability is the only way we can be reasonably sure that the people we're in relationship with are not suppressing in order to make things function. I'll be the first one to let you know that it won't always be easy to hear how your stress, insecurities, pride, or frustrations are negatively affecting the people in your life.

The question is, Would you rather hear about it or feel it in the way people slowly drift away? This process will make you vulnerable, and there will be moments when you even feel ashamed of the way you've acted or communicated. Once you survive the awkward vulnerability, you'll notice the roots of your relationship become deeper and richer.

Accountability produces an intimacy that can only be experienced when two individuals form a relationship where each is just as much teacher as they are student.

POWER FORWARD

I've only heard the phrase *power forward* used in basketball, but it's the two words that came to mind when deciding how to close this chapter. I'm not much of a basketball fan so I won't attempt to draw a parallel between the basketball position and the thought God gave me. So if you're a basketball fan I'm going to ask that you please forgive me in advance for deliberately expanding the definition to prove this next point.

It takes just as much power to be held accountable for the way that you cause harm as it does to move forward after you've been made aware of the ways you're still growing. Powering forward requires accepting the reality of your human frailty and being compassionate with yourself while maintaining your commitment to growth.

It's a little bit like rubbing your head and patting your stomach at the same time until you get into the rhythm of doing it. This is where stillness, intentional introspection, and an intimate prayer life become your healers and your weapons.

It's a weapon because it protects you from falling into an abyss of self-defeat, and it is your healer because it undergirds a message that you will have to learn over and over: you can be powerful without being perfect.

Introspection is when you take the time to examine your thoughts, emotions, and actions and recognize how they compete or align at any given moment. Through introspection we're able to understand that some of the ways we harm others are connected to unaddressed stress, fear, or anxiety.

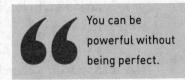

You can be powerful without being perfect.

Another person's feedback tells you what you did, but introspection helps you to understand how you were feeling and what you were thinking when you did it. I believe that introspection is a powerful tool when accompanied with prayer because it allows us to pour our hearts out to God.

It's one thing to pray about what you did, but it's another to ask God to help you heal and express the thoughts that allowed it to occur in the first place. You'll notice through introspection that you'll go from being defensive when someone attempts to hold you accountable to validating their experience because of the knowledge of the state you were in when the harm occurred.

The only way forward after you've caused harm is to reclaim the power of your weakness. You can allow your weakness to be what isolates and restricts you from connection, or you can see weakness as a runway.

There comes a moment when a plane is getting ready to take off where it seems like everything has come to a halt. The plane is aligned in the lane, passengers are buckled up, and the flight attendants have stopped moving about. If one didn't know any better, they wouldn't be able to tell if the plane has experienced some type of failure or if it's about to ascend to new heights. Those few seconds of stillness give way to the roar of engines, and suddenly the plane begins to move seemingly at full-throttle speed into the limitless sky.

When weakness becomes your runway, your only job is to hang tight to the truth that a momentary halt is not failure. It is your opportunity to recalibrate and rev up with more determination, focus, and power than you had before. I know you're probably wondering how it's even possible to accomplish such a task when the weight of your guilt, disappointment, or rejection feels too heavy to bear. I've got a scripture to help you with that.

It's 2 Corinthians 12:7–9 and it was written by the apostle Paul. He was sharing with a church in Corinth what Jesus said to him when he admitted to struggling with the fact that he was undeniably anointed and called. Yet on the other hand he was so well acquainted with his weakness that he called it a "thorn in the flesh" (v. 7).

This is how Paul said Jesus responded to his dilemma: "And He said to me, 'My grace is sufficient for you, for My strength is made perfect in weakness.'" Paul's response to the knowledge of Jesus' strength being made perfect in him is revealed in the second part of the verse when Paul shared, "Therefore most gladly I will rather boast in my infirmities, that the power of Christ may rest upon me" (v. 9).

When you're in that split second when weakness is threatening to make you feel like powering down altogether, I want you to remember this scripture. Remember that you can withstand the process of development that allows the power of Christ to rest upon you. Recognize that the promises of God over your life can only be voided if you allow your fear to cancel them out.

Don't allow the fact that you messed up to keep you down. If you're going to make a mistake, allow those moments to highlight just how far you are from being like God and how gracious God has been in extending you grace to make up the difference.

As a trauma survivor I have become passionate about normalizing accountability. I once felt that because I'd already learned a lot of difficult lessons I had no more room for messing up or making mistakes. The fear of being abandoned and rejected for disappointing others made it difficult for me to own my shortcomings and become better.

I was trying to preserve whatever power I thought was left after my mistakes. I didn't realize that my attempts at preserving power would rob me from receiving the power that is only available to those who move forward with Jesus' strength. I want my wounds to serve as wisdom for where you are on your journey.

> Brokenness and weakness may be the end of our tale in the eyes of some, but it will never be the end of our tale in God's eyes.

Accepting the dual nature of your existence as both victim and villain at any given moment makes room for you to wield your power with care and humility. Brokenness and weakness may be the end of our tale in the eyes of some, but it will never be the end of our tale in God's eyes.

If you're alive, the power of Christ can rest on you, imperfect as you may be, and make up the difference for the places where you fall short. I don't know who you may have harmed with your attitude, anger, frustration, stress, or disappointment, but I want to challenge you to not allow your pride to leave them wounded.

In your mind they may have deserved it for what they said or did, but no one should have enough power to pull you away from reflecting the image of God. Trust that even if they can't own the ways they've played a role in your harm, God knows how to avenge the heartbreak you've endured.

The best thing you can do with the grace you've been given is to focus on the ways you can grow.

Flip the Switch

MARINATE

When is the last time you offered someone an apology for your behavior? Explore whether the behavior is a recurring pattern that has shown up in your life before.

ACTIVATE

Give the people you're in relationship with a word or phrase to use when you're engaging in the harmful behavior you want to overthrow.

PRAY

God, my harm is powerful enough to ruin Your plan for my life. Help me to take seriously the ways that I need Your strength to partner with my weakness.

CHAPTER 17

SPREAD IT AROUND

WHEN I WAS GROWING UP I THOUGHT THAT HAVING CHILDREN WAS just about being able to say you have a family. My journey with parenting began when I was a teenager, so I learned on the job that parenting is really about raising future adults who love Jesus and are knowledgeable and confident enough to add indisputable value to their corner of the world.

Writing that sentence was much easier than actually raising these little crumb snatchers though. It's not any fault of their own but rather the reality of not always possessing the attributes I desire for them to have.

Sure, I want to move with power, burn with confidence, and become a force. One of the best ways to test whether that is happening is not judged in how frequently I embody that desire but how often I impart into others when I am functioning from that place. When you can't avoid the moments when you feel low, you must control what you impart from the place of despair.

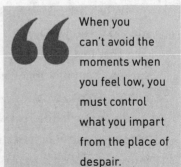

When you can't avoid the moments when you feel low, you must control what you impart from the place of despair.

· By now I hope you've been able to embrace the reality that power moves. Some days you feel unshakable and determined; other times you feel unmotivated and in shambles. That's normal, but part of knowing your harm is recognizing that in those moments what you share could be more than venting. It could actually be impartation.

Impartation is defined as "the act of imparting something (such as knowledge or wisdom)." The Latin etymology of the word *impart* indicates that the word means "in part."[13] This means that when we are sharing anything, whether it be knowledge or wisdom, we're not just venting to another person; we are giving them a part of what we're going through.

This is why it's so important to understand whether the person on the receiving end of our words is capable of processing what we share with empathy, wisdom, and discernment. Otherwise we'll be divulging a temporary frustration that has permanent implications because of who we gave a part of us.

This concept is made even clearer when we consider the ways that we must exhibit discretion when communicating with children, co-workers, or family members with misaligned core values and perspectives. Not every person in your life is in a position to carry your pieces with integrity.

If as much is true for the delicate parts of our lives, how much more truth does it hold for our ability to impart power? I'll take it a step beyond ability and say that it is our mandate to not just discover and harness our own power, but to make sure that we spread that power to others.

When Jesus first encountered a random man fishing in a sea, He didn't lure him away with promises of riches or fame. He didn't convince him that love and a pain-free life awaited him. Jesus simply made him curious about how following Him could awaken an identity that he didn't know he possessed.

How much different would the world be if each person who has been awakened and enlightened to the power they have to effect lasting divine impact made it their mission to awaken and enlighten others?

Changing how we think about power is doing the work so that we can understand the multidimensional ways we experience and express power and share our findings with others who feel powerless.

Don't gatekeep the areas where your power has been restored lest you become like those who've led so many to believe that power is only reserved for a select few. The real sign of someone who is confident is not how they walk into the room. It's how they change every room they walk into for the better.

If hurt people hurt people, then empowered people empower people. Sure enough, once Jesus awakened Peter to the potential lying dormant inside of him, we aren't just offered a glimpse of Jesus' journey as our Savior, but also of Peter's journey of receiving an impartation of Jesus' power.

Jesus did not limit or restrict His impartation based on a person's experience or worthiness. Jesus was not afraid that by imparting power He'd run low on it. He understood that the more power you possess, the more you have to give away. Power is not in limited supply, and when you truly trust your connection to the All-Powerful, you're not a hoarder of power who sees other people struggling but refuses to fill their cups.

JUMP START

When a car's battery has been drained, the owner has to find cables to hook the dead battery up to a full battery to get a charge. I remember sitting in the back seat of cars in my childhood while that transfer of power took place. The charged car would rev the engine until the car that was dead eventually came back to life.

Impartation is aligning where you're charged with the place where another person is drained. Now, before you start worrying about how you'll fit all of this into your already busy life, let me guide you on the best way to make this a part of your world.

When a car battery dies there are only two ways for another car to jump it. Another driver in proximity sees the struggling driver and asks if they can help by giving the car a jump. Or the person who needs a jump calls someone who can come to help them.

In either scenario there's one common denominator: proximity. That should be part of the criteria that we use to gauge our ability to impart the power we've received into someone else's life. Too often when we think about change and impact, we think about the people we may not yet know who could benefit from the grace on our lives.

This way of thinking discredits the opportunities that are in proximity for us to empower the people who are already in reach. You could be the spark someone needs to ignite their unique offering.

I've heard a few people tell me that they've known since they were young that they were gifted and special, but for the most part I hear testimonies of people who are wondering what sets them apart. They don't fully trust that there's anything about them that's worthy of distinction.

In the times of Jesus' life, being a fisherman was a common profession, but Jesus took what was common and bridged it to the supernatural. I bet Peter had no clue that his routine was actually the gateway for the supernatural.

I want to encourage you to begin asking God what He's placed inside of you that could be a jump start to a person in your community who is yet searching. Don't just take note of something that someone does well. Take the time to stress how special their offering is and how what they're calling their norm has greater impact than they realize.

You have to find a way to sow the power God's given you into the life of another person. Truly, Jesus shows us that power is not to be reserved but rather poured out into as many open and hungry vessels that one can reach.

Intentionally create opportunities for other people to grow and develop. Instead of teaching our children compliance, let's empower them to communicate their wants, needs, and frustrations. When you have the capacity, ask someone how you can use your resources to help them establish what God's doing in their life.

Locate the areas of your life where you have experienced the power of God in a way that feels unique. Then, like a car with a full battery, go and get next to someone who is dying in the place where you've been restored.

I'm ultimately admonishing you to go from being a seeker of power to a vessel of power. There comes a moment when you're not just going with the flow anymore. You've actually become the flow.

When someone encounters you, they're having a radical encounter with your authenticity and vulnerability. You should expect that you're carrying light with you wherever you go. You should not be surprised when people begin to say that they feel better, calmer, more hopeful once they've been in your presence.

That is the byproduct and overflow of what happens when we learn to seek the face of God and to project God's face in all that we see and do. Unleashing your light gives other people permission to do the same.

God has given us methods of communication to spread our power that don't even require us to go out of our way.

GIVE WITHIN REASON

In an attempt to secure individuality and distinction, I've noticed some people keeping their contacts, tips, and hacks to themselves. When you consider this from a professional perspective it makes sense. No one wants to work hard to build their business or career just to have someone imitate their gift and try to edge them out.

I do think it's necessary that we draw the line between having wisdom and being threatened by another person's growth. One of the ways that we can qualify whether someone is attempting to take advantage of their access to our power is to truly study them before imparting it.

Sometimes we are so busy trying to make sure that we pour into every person we meet that we don't take the time to observe if we're pouring into someone who is positioned to receive what we have to offer. When spreading power it's important to understand what the traits are of the person who can maximize the resource of you in their life.

Has the person demonstrated the ability to truly convert wisdom and knowledge from other sources in the past? If you're just getting to know someone more intimately, avoid giving them everything you have to offer at once. Only offer what you can afford to lose.

I cannot tell you how many times I've given someone the best of my thoughts, advice, and experiences only for them to do the direct opposite of what I'd suggested. I don't want to be one of those people who need others to respond the way that I see fit. My responsibility is to make sure that when I give, I'm able to give freely without being entitled to specific results.

If you're only investing in a person with the unspoken requirement that they will yield immediate transformation, it's actually manipulation. For the life of me I will never understand why God gave His only begotten Son so that "whosoever" believes in Him could have everlasting life.

If I gave my only child, you would *not* have an option on whether you believed. God demonstrates what it means to be a true giver. He gave His Son so that whosoever could have an option, not an obligation.

I think this speaks to the heart posture in which God gave and the same perspective we should imitate when giving. God gave because of who He is, not because of what He wanted in return. That's what I want for myself. That's what I want for you.

I want to be able to give because giving is who I am, not because giving is a means to an end. If you want this to be your truth, too, you must be willing to truly know the limits of what you can give without expecting anything in return, not even a thank-you.

What can you afford to give of yourself that you would give whether someone appreciated it or not? That's the beginning of setting the boundaries for how you engage with others. This does not mean that you don't give beyond that point, but it does mean that when you give beyond that point you should be considering what type of response or reaction makes you feel like your investment was truly valued.

Have you ever held the door open for someone to keep it from slamming in their face? Have you ever felt the anger of them not saying thank-you sting you in the moment?

> Your conviction to demonstrate kindness in that way has more to do with who you are than how they respond.

No matter how frustrated that may have made you, I bet it didn't deter you from holding the door open for someone else. You know why? Because your conviction to demonstrate kindness in that way has more to do with who you are than how they respond.

SOW THE SEED

I want to be clear: spreading power is not just something that has to involve you sharing the wisdom from some of your deepest wounds. You would be surprised how your norm could be empowering for someone else. Taking the time to make sure a person knows financial tools, communication tips, or time-saving practices that have helped you can serve them.

As a woman I find few things more powerful than another woman sharing with me how she's growing her hair, taking care of her skin, or finding time to practice self-care in her busy world. I won't even get into how we can serve one another when we share childcare contacts or educational ways to keep our children busy while we take time for ourselves.

The advantages of being in community with one another is that we have an opportunity to shorten the learning curve by sharing our experiences. You know you're truly confident when you're not threatened by someone else's access to what you have. At the end of the day someone having your recipe doesn't mean they'll get your results.

As we continue to see systems and structures crumble that historically excluded people groups, we must also confront the mentalities that made them successful in the first place. Subconsciously many of us have been engrained to believe that there can only be one of us in a space.

If we believe that there's only room for one woman, Black, Latina, young person, or old person, we do not actively seek to make room for others. There should be space for representation of all types at every table, and it shouldn't be limited to any one group feeling like a minority.

Dismantling the paradigm that there's only room for one helps us to be an active participant in creating space for the next wave of people to come. Jesus did what only He could do, then He got twelve disciples and gave them power, too, because the depravity of the world was so great that even as powerful as Jesus is, His impact would be multiplied by others.

When Jesus gave them a charge, among the many things He said, this stood out: "Heal the sick, cleanse the lepers, raise the dead, cast out demons. Freely you have received, freely give" (Matthew 10:7–8). Considering the strict systems of separation by class and ethnicity at the

> When God has granted you the ability to be powerful on Earth, it is not diminished by another person stepping into their power.

time, Jesus must have understood the human proclivity to absorb power for personal gain instead of spreading power for the uplifting of many. His warning gives us perspective on how we should respond to the opportunity to elevate another soul.

When God has granted you the ability to be powerful on earth, it is not diminished by another person stepping into their power. You must become an advocate with a mindset that says we need as many people to win as possible so that we can shine with brilliance into dark places. Lavishly share the hard-earned lessons you've learned with the people who are just starting off.

Do it because you recognize that the more people we sow into, the more opportunity we have for receiving a harvest of focused, intentional, and powerful beings. We cannot get a harvest where we have not planted seed. You want to see young people explore their passions and creativity? That's a great desire, but do you have any seed in the ground to back that desire up?

What changes do you want to see in your family, industry, friendships, or church? I bet you can create a long list of those things, but do you have any seed connected to that need?

I noticed a pet peeve in my organization that really got under my skin: In an effort to be nice, no one was direct. They would talk about "some member of the team" or about "some of the decisions that have been made." It frustrated me no end because I felt crippled as a leader without hard data. It didn't take me long to realize that the culture of communication was a direct reflection of how I communicate.

I was too worried about being nice and not worried enough about being effective. I didn't need to throw out one to have the other; I needed to find a way to marry the two. Not just for my sake, but for the people who were watching me. If I could demonstrate my power to do it, I could sow a seed by how they watch me so they could do the same.

Observation is impartation, whether it's with our children, team members, family, or friends. At the end of the day we are responsible for what we *do*, not what we meant and sometimes not even what we say.

First Samuel 16:7 says this much better than I do:

But the LORD said to Samuel, "Do not look at his appearance or at his physical stature, because I have refused him. For the LORD does not see as man sees; for man looks at the outward appearance, but the Lord looks at the heart."

It's not uncommon for this phrase to be used to justify the way we see people who look or dress differently than we do, but that's not the only thing we should be paying attention to when we see this. This verse gives us the cheat code for how people process and receive the way we show up in the world. If your outward presentation doesn't match your heart to see radical change take place in your relationships, profession, or community, then those around you will never have access to the inspiration that can make them better.

Flip the Switch

---------- **MARINATE** ----------

When is the last time you shared a treasured tip or trick with someone?

---------- **ACTIVATE** ----------

Choose a person who is growing in an area you've mastered, and make yourself available to impart knowledge, wisdom, and experience in their journey.

---------- **PRAY** ----------

God, help me to not become a hoarder of Your power out of fear of inadequacy. Position me to fill others up the areas where I have overflow.

CHAPTER 18

CLOSING OUT

I'M NOW THIRTY-FIVE YEARS OLD. ALTHOUGH IT FEELS LIKE I'VE LIVED a thousand lifetimes in those years, I'm hopeful that I still have a lot of living left. So, then, how does a woman who is still evolving leave you with a sense of staying power?

God gave me a clue.

Staying power is not about staying on "top," wherever that may be. It's not about outachieving yourself or those around you. Those definitions of staying power eventually leave us lonely and deflated.

Collins English Dictionary defines staying power as "the strength or determination to keep going until you reach the end of what you are doing."[14] *Merriam-Webster* says staying power is the "capacity for continuing (as in existence, influence, or popularity) without weakening."[15] When I read these definitions they each leave room for expiration. Merriam's depends on never weakening. It's humanly impossible to keep going physically without becoming weak. Collins's is intentional about adding an "end of what you are doing."

If you would allow me to merge the two definitions and leave you with something to ponder, I'll offer you this. Staying power is having the capacity to exercise strength or determination in trusting God without weakening. Power in the ways that I've hopefully unpacked for you is not about you at all; it's about living your life as an ode to the Most High.

> The only way any of us can truly stay powerful in the way that matters the most is to stay connected to the all-powerful, all-knowing, and ever-present God.

The only way any of us can truly stay powerful in the way that matters the most is to stay connected to the all-powerful, all-knowing, and ever-present God.

We're the only thing God has created that runs the risk of living without the original power God intended us to possess. The sun, ocean, moon, and stars still take their place each morning and evening. Some days their brightness is more luminous than others. In some seasons they're hardly detectable at all, but never do they cease to have power. I want you to know that staying power will look different from season to season.

If you're fortunate enough to experience the privilege of age, staying power is not about how much youth you can keep clenched in your grasp, nor is it about how those with you can accelerate maturation in an effort to achieve respect. Staying power is about having faith that believes that where you are, no matter how old or irrelevant it may seem, is not out of God's sight and can still be used for His plan.

When we make the destination of staying power about living authentically and actively seeking God's heart and perspective on our truth, it allows us the freedom to no longer pretend and removes the barrier, allowing us to lean in to how He may transform us. If you're going to finish strong at anything, you must stay connected to the ultimate Finisher. I don't know about you, but I don't want to finish as a hero in everyone else's eyes but be a failure at maximizing who God knew I could be.

It's especially hard for those of us who must analyze metrics to determine effectiveness. If your gauge for how effective or powerful you are is calculated with an algorithm, key performance indicators, reports, or feedback, you can easily fall into the trap of using someone else's criteria to determine your effectiveness. There are some careers where that cannot be avoided, but the metrics of your work, no matter how impressive or dismal, cannot determine the power of your being.

If the metrics of other people's opinions and thoughts are how you determine whether or not you're powerful, you'll run the risk of making acceptance and validation from others your finish line. Feedback without God as your filter can damage your soul and thwart your destiny. I have to remind myself to not be so focused on the metrics that determine impact in my world—as necessary and helpful as those might be—and dare to open my heart to becoming more sensitive to when God is challenging me to remember that who I am is more important than what I can offer.

It's not always easy, but my anxiety gives me a clue. It's how I can tell that I'm out of authenticity and have moved into relentless productivity. I have come to recognize that pressure and stress are byproducts of a belief system, and I weigh whether the goal of that system is to make me a great performer or a better person. The only staying power worth seeking is God's endorsement staying on my life. I'm hoping that this message will be a gift to you, yes, but above all I want it to be an offering to Him. A reflection of my heart to position those He loves towards knowing Him and the highest version of themselves more deeply.

Just in case finishing strong for you has always been about measuring quantifiable outcomes or receiving feedback from those you're in relationship with, I want you to consider something. If there were no report to review and the mouths that surrounded you were muted, how would you know in your soul that you finished strong? As a parent, partner, friend, sibling, child, or colleague, how would you know? When life inevitably turns the page from one role to the next, how will you know that you've walked away with power from that stage as opposed to losing your power in the transition?

I'll give you what God gave me.

Anytime you finish with a lesson that helps you see yourself more clearly and trust God more completely, you have finished strong. You're probably going through the catalog of your mind right now determining how many finishes resulted in a lesson that holds power. Guess what? Even if you have unfinished business from transitions that left you feeling powerless, know that revenge is not a medium for power—it's an abuse of it—but perspective is. It's not too late to find the lesson and discover the strength to live again.

There is one final indicator of a life that finishes strong: trusting that doing it the way God has ordered, no matter how unique, is the only path to ultimate freedom. Find your confidence to be authentic. Trust that you can effect change. Don't you dare get stuck in stagnancy, and do all that you can to ask for help when you've gone astray. Keep your heart open to the impossible, and trust that you have the endurance to withstand the inevitable fears that come when you move the way that power moves.

Hope to see you in the flow.

ACKNOWLEDGMENTS

FEW THINGS MAKE ME FEEL AS POWERFUL AS THE TIMES WHEN I'VE created a safe space for my husband and children to be vulnerable and honest with me. The honor of hearing their dreams and shining a light into their fears makes my heart smile. If my life had a pit stop where I could go from low-power mode to fully charged in a matter of seconds, I'd name it Touré Roberts and look for it everywhere I go.

I love that this message on the fluidity of power was formed as I navigated our children through six very different seasons of life. Each of them needing something different from me gave me the depth and courage to trust the power of this book. Ren, Ty, Teya, Chi, Isaiah, Makenzie, and Ella: you can always count on me to flow with you when you need me and to fall back when it's time for you to move at the speed of your destiny.

Beyond my husband, children, and family of origin, there is one space where I deeply treasure witnessing the power of God flow, and that's at Woman Evolve. Whether the flow is working on our internal structure and team to help us better reflect the values we espouse to others, through our content, or in a room with thousands, we have experienced the undeniable reassurance of God partnering with our work to change lives. Sometimes I think about the moment when power will move and the work that we do will be antiquated compared to the innovation of another generation, and I get joy thinking of the path we're blazing with them in mind.

I'm grateful to the delegation of Woman Evolve for trusting that my relationship with God could help them with their own. I don't take the honor of serving you lightly. Your love has served as confirmation from God in the moments when I've needed it the most. I can't wait to keep growing in love, grace, and power with you.

Vonetta and Bey, I could not ask for a better support system. I'm so grateful for the ways you've covered me so that I could break down, rebuild, and emerge again. Elisha, thank you for attempting to make the work look easy. I know it's not. I pray you reap on the level you sowed. Our team at Woman Evolve is ridiculously small and supernaturally gifted. The generosity you've granted me does not go unnoticed. Your patience is not in vain. I'm becoming better with you in mind.

Shannon and Jan, the best to ever do it. Ten years later and you're still showing me the power of what pages bound together can do to awaken healing and spur restoration.

Our church family from LA to Dallas and the faithful e-members have shown me the power of community gathering to change a generation. Praying that each of you will get caught in the current of purpose and leave God's mark on you in the earth.

God, I pray the words on these pages have in some way cleared the lens that keeps us from seeing the way we bear Your image. May the meditation of my heart and words of my mouth be pleasing and acceptable in Your sight. I'm grateful that You would allow me to serve this generation. Keep my heart open and tender to move with Your power no matter where it takes me.

NOTES

1. *Oxford English Dictionary*, s.v. "power," accessed November 2, 2023, https://oed.com/search/dictionary/?scope=Entries&q=power.
2. *Merriam-Webster*, s.v. "empowered," accessed November 2, 2023, https://merriam-webster.com/dictionary/empowered.
3. *Strong's Definitions from Strong's Concordance*, s.v. "châzaq (ḥāzaq)," on Blue Letter Bible, accessed November 2, 2023, https://blueletterbible.org/lexicon/h2388/kjv/wlc/0-1.
4. Youmatter, "Ecosystems: Definition, Examples, and Importance—All About Ecosystems," modified February 17, 2020, https://youmatter.world/en/definition/ecosystem-definition-example.
5. *Online Etymology Dictionary*, s.v. "disappoint,", accessed November 2, 2023, https://etymonline.com/word/disappoint.
6. "About," BuyNothing, accessed November 2, 2023, https://buynothingproject.org/about.
7. *Merriam-Webster*, s.v. "subdue," accessed November 2, 2023, https://merriam-webster.com/dictionary/subdue.
8. Cultish Creative, "Esther Perel's (Gangster) Confidence Definition," *Cultish Creative* (blog), April 13, 2021, https://cultishcreative.com/esther-perels-gangster-confidence-definition.
9. Educational Resources, "Find-a-Feature: Confluence," US Geological Survey, accessed November 2, 2023, https://usgs.gov/educational-resources/find-feature-confluence.
10. "Solimãµes-Negro River Confluence at Manaus, Amazonia," Images, NASA Earth Observatory, July 7, 2004, https://earthobservatory.nasa.gov/images/5254/solimaes-negro-river-confluence-at-manaus-amazonia.

11. Guihyun Park, Beng-Chong Lim, and Hui Si Oh, "Why Being Bored Might Not Be a Bad Thing After All," *Academy of Management Discoveries* 5, no. 1 (March 26, 2019), https://journals.aom.org/doi/10.5465/amd.2017.0033.

12. *Encyclopaedia Britannica Online*, eds., s.v. "Hippocratic oath," Brittanica, updated October 13, 2023, https://britannica.com/topic/Hippocratic-oath.

13. *Merriam-Webster*, s.v. "impartation," accessed October 22, 2023, https://merriam-webster.com/dictionary/impartation.

14. *Collins English Dictionary*, s.v. "staying power," accessed October 22, 2023, https://collinsdictionary.com/us/dictionary/english/staying-power.

15. *Merriam-Webster*, s.v. "staying power," accessed October 22, 2023, https://merriam-webster.com/dictionary/stayingpower.

ABOUT THE AUTHOR

SARAH JAKES ROBERTS IS AN AUTHOR, SPEAKER, ENTREPRENEUR, and philanthropist. She is the founder of Woman Evolve, a multimedia platform that provides women with the tools, support, and encouragement necessary to make positive and lasting changes. Through various resources such as digital and live events, books, podcasts, and online content, Woman Evolve seeks to address the holistic needs of women and empower them to lead fulfilling and impactful lives.

Alongside her husband, Touré Roberts, Sarah copastors at ONE Los Angeles and serves in leadership at The Potter's House Dallas. Her messages spread throughout the world, defying cultural, religious, gender, and socioeconomic boundaries. With her down-to-earth personality, contemporary style, and revelatory messages, there's no question why Time100 Next named her an emerging thought leader for this generation.